Pleasures
of *the*
Cottage
Garden

Pleasures
of the
Cottage
Garden

RAND B. LEE

FRIEDMAN/FAIRFAX
PUBLISHERS

A FRIEDMAN/FAIRFAX BOOK

©1998 by Michael Friedman Publishing Group, Inc.

Library of Congress Cataloging-in-Publication data available upon request.

ISBN 1-56799-695-7

Editors: Susan Lauzau and Elizabeth Helfgott
Art Director: Jeff Batzli
Designer: Orit Tenzer
Photography Editors: Deidra Gorgos and Jennifer L. Bove
Production Manager: Susan Kowal

Color separations by Radstock Repro
Printed in England by Butler & Tanner Limited

1 3 5 7 9 10 8 6 4 2

For bulk purchases and special sales, please contact:
Friedman/Fairfax Publishers
Attention: Sales Department
15 West 26th Street
New York, New York 10010
212/685-6610   FAX 212/685-1307

Visit our website:
http://www.metrobooks.com

FOR MOTHER AND JEFF

CONTENTS

INTRODUCTION

FOUR COTTAGE GARDENS

"Show me your garden and
I shall tell you what you are."

—ALFRED AUSTIN,

THE GARDEN THAT I LOVE (1905)

Cottage gardening as a conscious design style is a child of eighteenth- and nineteenth-century Western romanticism, attempting to recapture, as it does, in its slightly superior way, the largely imaginary good old days of bucolic English village innocence. But a kind of cottage gardening has been practiced for centuries all over the world, wherever there were people who wanted to grow flowers or vegetables near their homes, the better to protect and care for them. However, for all practical purposes, what English-speaking people today call "cottage gardening" borrows heavily from British folkways, and it is this tradition more than any other that is reflected in this book.

To me, the cottage garden is an informal series of plantings, featuring ornamentals or edibles or both, designed to avoid a show of wealth and located near the gardener's dwelling. By "informal" I mean that the cottage garden must not look micromanaged, with every bud and tendril in its place; the look should be soft and spreading rather than rigid and controlled. Paths should be wide enough for easy strolling and wheelbarrowing. And the garden *must* include plants that hold a strong positive emotional association for the gardener. So although a modern cottage garden may include the very latest 'Fluffy Ruffles' rhododendron from the most up-to-date nursery, it ought also to give special place to Great

Grandma Betsy's penguin gourd vine and that hideous hydrangea Uncle Bill so cherished. Some cottage gardeners take this one step further, and permit only old-fashioned, open-pollinated, "heirloom" or "passalong" plants in their carefully dug beds. There is also an increasing tendency among North American enthusiasts to emphasize in their cottage gardens plants that are native or long-adapted to their local areas.

Pots, urns, half-barrels, birdbaths, bird feeders, gazebos, garden arches, recycling fountains shaped like wee boys urinating, freestanding greenhouses, patios, gazing-globes, tables, chairs, plastic crocodiles, dials declaring only the sunny hours, and garden seats may also crop

In early summer, the garden blooms with poppies (*Papaver* spp.), catmint (*Nepeta* x *faaseni*), lupines (*Lupinus* spp.), fennel (*Foeniculum vulgare*), and several types of alliums. Opposite, a classic garden bench beckons visitors down the path, encouraging them to stay awhile.

up in such gardens, but only the last is a requirement. The cottage garden must invite entry, and nothing invites entry as much as a nice, sturdy, comfortable seat strategically placed.

I have known intimately four cottage gardens, one located in New England, one in southern Florida, one in Ireland, and one in New Mexico. I would like to tell you a bit about them, since they illustrate just how elastic the term "cottage garden" can be.

The first cottage garden I ever encountered was my mother's. We lived on sixty-three and a half acres (25.5ha) in rural Connecticut, and in the 1950s, when I was a child, Connecticut was very rural indeed. My father was a detective novelist who worked from home; my mother was a retired character actress whose peripatetic childhood had primed her for the pleasures of staying in one place long-term. Our house and land had been part of an estate at the turn of the century. Wisely, my mother did no planting until the first spring; she wanted to see what gardeners before her had done before she put her personal stamp on

All-white gardens are hopelessly fashionable today, and I do admit their charms, but Mother loathed them. The first chance she got, she planted bright perennials, like the phlox (*Phlox paniculata* 'Balmoral') below.

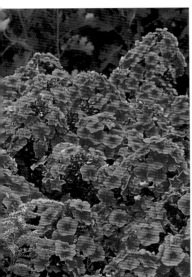

things. She was aghast, therefore, when come April and May, she discovered that every perennial, bulb, and shrub near the house bloomed white. Nowadays white gardens are fashionable, but to Mother, an all-white garden was funereal. In later years she relished relating how she had ripped out every pallid

offender and replaced them with proper plants; but although Mother was opinionated, she was no fool. She left numerous stands of white violets, a colony of snowdrops near our neighbors' fence, some gloriously fragrant mock oranges at the back of Dad's study, some snowball bushes near the screened-in porch, a

noble white dogwood, and a beautiful white bridal veil spirea.

She also planted hollyhocks and gladioli near the barn, strawberries off the driveway, hostas ("funkias" to her) and tall garden phloxes near the well house, and rhubarb next to the horse corral. Around the maple tree in

Hollyhocks (*Alcea* spp.) are edible relatives of cotton (*Gossypium* spp.) and okra (*Abelmoschus esculentus*). Where rust fungus mars your hollyhocks, try substituting some pretty (if slightly less stately) relatives: the tree mallows (*Lavatera* spp.); the dwarfish *Malope trifida*; the prairie mallows (*Sidalcea* spp.); or, of course, the various hibiscuses (*Hibiscus* spp.).

the ell of the house she grew wax begonias in pots. In an oval plot shaded by the white dogwood (which she insisted was sacred and should never be cut for house decoration) she planted columbines, blue violets, bleeding-hearts, and one hundred tall bearded iris rhizomes, which bloomed for many years in every imaginable hue. These irises had been a gift of Rex Stout, the late mystery novelist, brother to Ruth Stout, the no-dig mulch queen. I can remember the day she put them in the ground, because our pet albino turkey, Horatio, followed her around the garden, sticking his head into each hole she made, inspecting her efficiency.

Of course we had roses. Some were growing wild on the property already. Some double, deep red, pepper-scented ones grew in back of the pony corral; and at the edge of our woods there were single-flowered, white multifloras, their honey scent so attractive that Mother forgave them their invasiveness and planted more along the driveway. But her favorite roses were the hybrid teas. She ordered them by mail from Jackson & Perkins, and planted a bunch of them in the backyard, not far from the porch where the snowball bushes made their poppable fruits. The three she treasured the most were the dayglo orange 'Tropicana', deep red 'Mister Lincoln', and the

queen of them all, 'Peace', which in those days had a sweet perfume.

Mother had a vegetable garden, too. It took up a third of an acre, at least, tilled from virgin grassland and enriched with wheelbarrow load after wheelbarrow load of aged horse, cow, and sheep manure. It was out of sight of the main house; in designing it thus, Mother was unconsciously following ancient tradition, for English cottage gardeners very frequently separated their edibles from their ornamentals, and still do. (The French tend to mix them, a style I prefer.) The sheer volume of food Mother coaxed from this plot staggers my mind. Everything was from open-pollinated seed except for the raspberry bushes and the 'Martha Washington' asparagus (the smell of which, steaming, would draw like a magnet all seven of our cats). We had English peas, which never made it to table, and endless rows of snap beans in green and yellow. We had spinach and summer squash coming out of our ears. We had 'Connecticut Field' pumpkins. We had 'Country Gentleman' sweetcorn. And we had tomatoes, rich glossy monsters, both a yellow kind, the name of which I never knew, and the original 'Beefsteak' (also called 'Crimson Cushion'). One year we had so many tomatoes that, having canned hundreds of jars of tomato puree and having given away wheelbarrows full of the fresh fruit to all our neighbors, Mother

Fresh summer squash, above, is a gardener's delight. A cherry tomato, right, is cunningly displayed. Tomatoes and roses enjoy exactly the same conditions in which to thrive: full sun; regular water; deep, rich, slightly acidic soil; and daily attention from folk in garden clothes.

decreed the leftover crop artillery. My older brothers used them up in great and glorious battle, much to the delight of the dogs.

I have never made a garden as successful as my mother's. For one thing, I have never owned my own land, and for another, I am extraordinarily lazy, something my mother was not. But after I had finished college and tasted my fill of the urban world, I returned to my mother's house and made a kind of cottage garden there.

The garden I made was in the backyard of my mother's new house on the island of Key West, Florida, the southernmost island in the Florida Keys. She had been forced to sell the Connecticut property after the death of my father, and I think the sadness we felt for the

loss of it was mixed up somehow with our sadness for the loss of him. At any rate, Key West's supertropical climate and barren, coral-based soil was a far cry from Connecticut's temperate loam. I was in my early thirties when I joined Mother and my brother Jeff at their house on Higgs Lane, and during the six years we all lived together, I learned how to garden all over again.

Half of the Higgs Lane garden was the province of Jeff and Mother, a lovely cool courtyard set with a trickling fountain and neatly kept tropical shrubs. My half was weedy and neglected. While Mother and Jeff fooled around with hibiscuses, hoyas, and hot-house orchids (all of which grow outdoors in

How very annoying to find greenhouse treasures thriving like dandelions in Key West's Zone 11 climate.

Clockwise from top: hybrid hibiscus (*Hibiscus* spp.), *Hoya carnosa*, and the orchid *Cymbidium* 'Hurrah'.

Key West with practically no care), I decided I was going to homestead. It was the first time I had ever tried to grow food. There were some valuable fruit trees on the site already. A loquat, the fruit of which tastes like a combination of lemon and cherry, hung over the driveway fence, and a sapodilla, which makes fuzzy brown balls that soften to a brown sugar flavor and texture, grazed the roof from its spot in our neighbor's yard. To these I added a Barbados cherry, which yields tiny, sour, ribbed, tomato red, vitamin-rich acerola berries; a dwarf banana palm, which eventually produced huge, heroic hands of small, reddish-skinned, apple custard–flavored bananas; a tomato patch (in containers on the sitting room roof); and a bed of cantaloupes, which I started on the big compost heap I engineered. The tomatoes and melons I grew from seed were reputed to be especially bred for tropical conditions, and I was delighted when they produced reasonable crops with no sign of mildew.

If you have never gardened in a frost-free region, you are missing treasures beyond the wildest dreams of avarice. Where else could you weed the tropical melon patch to the wafted scent of the perfume acacia? Or descale an outdoor stephanotis vine, heavy with waxy, scented blossoms? Where else could you watch a passionflower take over a roof in one season? I will never forget the thrill of cutting that first hand of bananas, or the apple-custard taste of them, or the look on my mother's face when she sampled our first melon. When she finally sold the Higgs Lane house, we all felt that we had left it better than we had found it, and were content.

The third cottage garden I made was in County Cork, Ireland. My Anglophilic mother and brother, who had tried to emigrate to England from Key West, had been kicked out after a year (they had no relatives there to plead their case to the immigration authorities), so they had shunted themselves westward to emerald Eire. It was to be their last home. I visited them with my friend Alex the next winter. We stayed for four months. I was

Exotic passionflowers of all kinds are easy to grow in the semitropical Florida Keys. The cultivar 'Maypop', right, can be grown further north, as it is hardy to Zone 6. Opposite, in classic cottage fashion, the climbing rose 'Zephirine Drouhin' and the starry flowers of *Clematis montana* 'Alba' garland an English facade.

It is essential that the cottage garden invite entry. Rustic gates, crumbling stone walls, and bursts of half-barreled floristry don't hurt a bit.

itching to leave my mark on the property. Jeffrey, whose tastes were a trifle Jekyllian, had done wonders with conifers, red hot pokers, pampas grass (his addiction), and the inevitable yuccas, but I wanted a proper cottage garden, and so (it developed) did Mother.

In the end, Alex and I carved out a twenty by fifty-foot (6 by 15m) bed from the stony acid turf downslope of the main house. The turves we dug out we used to build a stairway up the steep hill-grade from the garden to the upper terrace where the house stood. We double dug the poor soil, manuring and liming it within an inch of its life, and somehow managed to create a series of perennial beds ringed by hybrid tea roses and stocked with all the

English cottage garden staples: delphiniums and lupines, true English daisies, orange-red geums, seed-grown columbines, crocosmias, irises, wee saxifrages, dahlias, foxgloves, forget-me-nots, pansies, and mother-of-thyme. Alex and I left Ireland before we could see the planting mature, but Mother sent me photos the next year, and I was astonished at how established and natural the garden appeared. Alex was unsurprised. "It's the little people," he explained. "They liked us."

Of course, Mother extended the plot, adding rows of raspberries and gooseberries and a small stand of dwarf fruit trees. Jeff added a covered garden seat, planted a golden chain tree up the slope, and expanded the

dahlias into a bed of their own nearer the sitting room window. His final contribution was the planting of a white oak and a copper beech at the back of the garden near the old holly. When his dog Jespah died of old age, Jeff buried him at the foot of the oak. After Jeff in his turn died of AIDS, and Mother followed him through grief a year later, I went back to the garden and sat in the evening, feeling the peace my loved ones had left, as the seals barked in the bay.

My fourth garden, here in Santa Fe, is worlds apart from all the others. Here, at 7,000 feet (2,134m) above sea level, I contend with heavy alkaline clay, 8.0-plus on the pH scale. Annual rainfall averages about fifteen to twenty

Sweet Williams (*Dianthus barbatus*) and common hyacinths (*Hyacinthus orientalis*) are enormously adaptable, thriving (on a drip line) even in Santa Fe's alkaline clay.

inches (38 to 51cm); the humidity ranges from 15 to 45 percent (in a wet summer). When I rented this house at 1306 Lujan Street in the autumn of 1989, the backyard was concrete hardpan and waist-high weeds, the victim of ten years' neglect, though I did find, around the gutter downspout, a determined patch of peppermint, daylilies, and (of all things) bladder campions. I recognized the campions at once: they had been common wildflowers on our land in Connecticut when I was a boy.

I took it as a good omen. The next spring I started my first flower bed, hacking it out of the clay, fertilizing with bagged steer manure (quite innocent of the salinizing effect it would have on the already hopeless soil). I planted lavender, watered it unfaithfully, and found, to my delight, that it thrived. Then I read Penelope Hobhouse and longed for a healthy stand of Himalayan blue poppies, but I recognized that the world holds only a few spots where anything like a true British climate may be found, and I knew that it would be folly for me to try to copy a true English cottage garden under my high arid, juniper-pinon belt conditions. But I did not want to give up English flowers entirely. So I adopted a try-it-thrice strategy. I decided that if I killed something three times, I would not attempt it again. Hoping to minimize my expenses, I pestered the local nursery folk for ideas, and combed the garden encyclopedias for mention of any flowers that tolerated clay, chalk, or drought.

Eight years later, with the help of mulch and soaker hoses, my cottage garden grows many familiar cottage flowers: crocuses, hyacinths, tulips, daffodils, lilacs, calendulas, pinks, baby's-breath, bachelor's buttons, sweet Williams, sweet scabious, morning glories, jasmine tobacco, zinnias, lilybells, platycodons, and sunflowers. I have also learned to appreciate the merits of both southwestern U.S. natives and drought-adapted variants of common English plants: I am giving more and more space to our local penstemons, to the agastaches, to Mexican salvias, to ornamental alliums, to California epilobiums, to species tulips

(which evolved under dry conditions), and to drought-tolerant fruits such as golden currant (*Ribes aureum*) and 'Regent' saskatoon. On the other hand, the garden still lacks many British essentials. I grow no primulas, no astilbes, no saxifrages, no corydalis, and only one foxglove (a pale straw yellow, *Digitalis lutea*). I grow only five roses: 'Tiffany', a hybrid tea (in memory of Mother); *Rosa alba* 'Semiplena', the white rose of York, which doubles in size every year with minimal care; *Rosa* × *damascena* 'Quatres Saisons', which blooms slightly chlorotically spring and autumn (it is luscious for potpourri); an Austin English rose, 'William Shakespeare' (which needs lots of water); and the effortlessly easy gold-and-tomato 'Austrian Copper' rose (also known as *Rosa foetida* var. *bicolor*).

I find that I cannot grow melons, squash, cucumbers, or garden hollyhocks; they all succumb to mildew, grasshoppers, and a particularly noxious variety of leaf-eating cutworm, which devours what the mildew and grasshoppers do not. The grasshoppers I have learned to control with bran bait inoculated with a fatal grasshopper disease (it is marketed under the names Nolo and Semaspore); the cutworms I

A look of artless chaos is what you want in a cottage garden, with as much variety as possible. Here, a jumble of reds and pinks offers a refreshing departure from the usual tasteful pastels.

Learning the plants that will thrive in your area and planning your cottage garden around them will make your life much easier. The penstemons, veronicas, and campanulas growing in the border opposite are notoriously hearty. If you simply must grow a particular plant, consider constructing a raised bed or putting it in a container, where you can better control its growing conditions.

drown in embryo by watering the garden heavily in October, when the mommies lay their eggs. But I have given up on cucurbits and hollyhocks. The wild hollyhocks growing out of cracks in pavement near the local car wash are much prettier and healthier than anything I could manage, and the local farmers' market offers ambrosial melons and cucumbers at a tenth of what it would cost me in labor and chemicals to grow them myself.

Now some of my Santa Fe gardening acquaintances (I hesitate to call them "friends") look bewildered when I tell them my tales of woe. "Why," said one gentleman to whom I no longer speak, "my 'Excelsior' foxgloves are taking over the garden!" Nevertheless, it is my opinion that one must accept one's limitations and the limitations of one's ecosystem. If you yearn for a proper English cottage garden but you do not live in England (or some place like

it), I advise you to ask yourself how you can use native or locally adapted plants to get the look, scent, and feel you want.

And of course you may read this book. In the following pages you will find shrubs, vines, annuals, perennials, biennials, roots, tubers, and the occasional tomato, all demonstrated to be foolproof and just right for the cottage garden. Do not ask who the fool was who proved them. I daresay you can guess.

CHAPTER ONE

THE ROOTS OF COTTAGE GARDENING

Lord Illingsworth: The Book of Life begins with
a man and a woman in a garden.
Mrs. Allonby: It ends with Revelations.
—OSCAR WILDE, *A WOMAN OF NO IMPORTANCE*

The cottage garden is generally thought of as a flower garden, and perhaps that is true as cottage gardens are conceived of today. But originally, ornamentals were the least important denizens of the cottage plot.

One of the earliest descriptions of a real cottage garden—that is, a garden really designed and managed by a cottage-dweller who depended upon it for at least some of his subsistence—is found in *Account of a Cottage and Garden near Tadcaster*, an English pamphlet published in 1797 by Thomas Bernard, quoted in Anne Scott-James's *The Cottage Garden*. Bernard writes:

Two miles from Tadcaster, on the left-hand side of the road to York, stands a beautiful little cottage, with a garden that has long attracted the eye of the traveler. The slip of land is exactly a rood [about a quarter of an acre], inclosed by a cut quick hedge; and containing the cottage, fifteen apple-trees, one green gage, and three wine-sour plum trees, two apricot-trees, several gooseberry and currant bushes, abundance of common vegetables, and three hives of bees; being all the apparent wealth of the possessor.

Flowers are not mentioned at all. This does not mean that none were grown; it may mean merely that they were not considered worthy of including in the list of "the apparent wealth of the possessor" of the garden. But there is some evidence for believing that flowers were not as important to early cottage gardens as they became to later ones.

Early Evidence

It is thought that medieval cottage gardens, from which modern cottage gardens descend, were essentially fenced-in yards with shed and mobile privy, arranged to enclose and protect the all-important family food animals: cows, pigs, and chickens. They may also have held a few fruit trees, medicinal herbs, and basic veg-

The earliest cottage gardens appear to have been gardens "for meat and medicine," granting the householder more power over his or her food supply. Food security permitted cultivation of flowers for their own sakes.

A mixed planting of herbs, left, includes flowering alliums, purple sage, and lady's mantle. Gardeners throughout the ages have included medicinal plants in their cottage plots. Below, 'Early Pear' tomato ripens in the September sun. Tomatoes were originally grown by the British as ornamentals.

etables. It is difficult to know for certain, because most medieval records describe the gardens of the wealthy. Not until the sixteenth century do we find anything like a detailed description of what ordinary people really grew and ate and admired.

Thomas Tusser's best-selling *A Hundred Good Points of Husbandry* (1557) describes—in end-rhyming verse—a cottage garden and orchard on a small but reasonably prosperous working Tudor farm. The farmer's wife is in charge of this garden, in which Tusser records growing a galaxy of herbs, both medicinal and culinary; salad greens and vegetables; and ornamentals for cutting and container-growing. Soft fruits and stone fruits were grown at this period, and bees were kept as well.

During the reign of Elizabeth I, new prosperity brought into England foreign fashions in gardening and cookery, as hundreds of new ornamentals and edibles were being imported from the Americas and the East. Gardening became so much the fashion among the aristocracy (and hence, by trickle-down, to the new middle classes) that by 1629 herbalist John Parkinson had a bestseller in his *Paradisi in Sole, Paradisus Terrestris*, the first major English gardening book devoted to recreational (rather than subsistence) horticulture. In it Parkinson describes as suitable to the home garden an orgy of flowers, herbs, fruits, and vegetables, many of them named cultivars and many of them still grown today.

There are some surprising omissions. The potato, sweet potato, and Jerusalem artichoke are discussed as little more than curiosities. So is the tomato, the most grown vegetable in home gardens today. Parkinson places it in his flowers section under "Pomum Amoris, Love Apples," saying apologetically, "Although the beautie of this plant consisteth not in the flower, but fruit, yet give me leave to insert it here, lest otherwise it have no place." He describes only three kinds of tomatoes: one "the bignesse of a small...Pippin," pale to deeper red, "like unto an Orenge"; a pale yellow variant; and a kind bearing very small yellowish red fruits, which he has known to self-sow in his garden. Interestingly, the normally vigilant Parkinson says nothing about love apples being poisonous (a common belief); on the contrary, he notes that "in the hot Countries where they naturally growe, they are much eaten of the people, to coole and quench the heate and thirst of their hot stomaches." But he is silent about their suitability for the English stomach, and the fact that it never occurred to him to list them in the kitchen garden section suggests that tomatoes were not eaten by his English contemporaries.

Garden Plants Known by 1629

(From John Parkinson, *Paradisi in Sole, Paradisus Terrestris*)

Apples (over 56 kinds)
Apricots ("apricockes," 6 kinds)
Beans
Beets, white, green, yellow,
    and red
Carnations
Cherries (35 kinds)
Cowslips
Cucumbers
Currants, red, white, and black
Daffodils
Dame's-rocket
Daylilies
English daisies
Foxgloves
Gooseberries, red, blue, and green

Grapes (23 kinds)
Hellebores
Hyacinths
Irises
Jasmines
Lettuces (10 kinds, 2 of them
    red)
Lilacs
Lilies
Lungworts
Melons
Monkshoods
Nectarines (6 kinds, including
    the musk nectarine, which
    "both smelleth and eateth
    as if the fruit were
    steeped in Muske")

Onions
Oxlips
Parsnips
Passionflowers
Peaches (23 kinds)
Pears (over 64 kinds, including
    a striped kind and a musk-
    flavored kind)
Peas
Peonies
Pinks
Plums (62 kinds, including the
    rare striped "white diapred
    plum of Malta")
Poppies
Primroses

Raspberries,
    white and red
Roses (many)
Salad greens (numerous)
Stocks
Strawberries
Sunflowers
Sweet Williams
Thorn-apples
Tulips ("Tulipas" or "Turks'
    Caps", 41 kinds)
Turnips
Violets
Wallflowers

TULIP

IRIS

The Artisan Florists

By 1667, the gardening fashion had spread throughout most of southern England, and the first florists' societies were being formed. "Florists" were flower breeders, usually men (or at least it is the men who find their way into the extant records), frequently working-class and artisans, who by selecting seed from favored plants and deliberate hybridization set out to improve their favorite garden flowers. The various societies were fiercely competitive, awarding prizes for those flowers that met exhaustingly stringent standards of geometric and aesthetic perfection. In time, florists came to categorize some flowers as "in" and some flowers as "out," thus creating that enduring archetype, the Garden Snob.

It is important to note that florists, cottagers, and cottage gardens were by no means confined to the countryside. As garden historian Anne Scott-James points out, from medieval times until the late eighteenth century, the term "cottager" referred not only to "the small farmer or husbandman, the country craftsman, especially the blacksmith,...and any servants of the gentry who 'lived out,'" but also to town-dwelling cottagers, such as "the town artisan, if he had his own small plot." Furthermore, many of these people, like the Tadcaster gardener described previously, did not own the land they gardened, but leased it from an estate owner. Modern urbanites and renters therefore have as much historical right to lay claim to the cottage gardening tradition as anybody.

In the eighteenth century, due in part to sanctions by the British Parliament and in part to the burgeoning landscape garden movement, many cottagers were turned out of their rented homes or had the land around their cottages confiscated by landlords caught up in the fashion for enclosing portions of their estates and making parks out of them. However, the florists' societies and the small farmers still existed to keep cottage gardening alive, and some socially conscious gentry began to build model villages across Britain,

This dooryard arrangement of cottage flowers, so charming to us, might have been considered rather low-status by the perfectionistic florist breeder of the eighteenth century.

complete with built-in cottage plots for flowers, fruits, and vegetables. Near the end of the century, many aristocrats, fallen on hard economic times, themselves turned to cottage living, popularizing it still further in the public imagination.

By the first quarter of the nineteenth century, what Anne Scott-James calls "the two streams of cottage gardening, romantic gardening and subsistence gardening," had joined. Two basic garden designs proliferated, and they were subject to endless variation, ranging in size from a quarter of an acre (about one-tenth of a hectare)—considered the ideal—to many times that, as orderly or chaotic as individual cottagers' tastes dictated.

In the first layout, the cottage was built close to the road, with a narrow hedge-bordered flower plot in front, potted plants on the windowsills, and a larger area in the back for vegetables, livestock, and garden maintenance accoutrements. In the second design, the cottage was set back from the road, with a flower-bordered vegetable garden in front bisected by a path leading from the road to the front door. The back was reserved for animals and accoutrements alone. Fruit trees, climbing vines, bee skeps, and perhaps a well or pond might complete the picture.

By late century, many Victorian writers, architects, artists, and gardeners had taken up the cottage garden ideal as symbolic of the

romantic joys of voluntary simplicity, the hardworking happy peasant life, and what today might be termed "family values." William Robinson's *The English Flower Garden* came out in 1883; many historians call it one of the most influential gardening books ever published. The Parkinson Society, an organization founded to rescue old cottage garden plant varieties, was begun in the 1880s by one Mrs. Ewing, who also wrote several books romanticizing the cottage gardening style; Mrs. C.W. Earle (*Pot Pourri from a Surrey Garden*, 1897) wrote nostalgically of gardening in the 1840s and 1850s. After the turn of the century, English garden designer Gertrude Jekyll and architect Edwin Lutyens reinterpreted the

A true garden idyll: waterlilies, red *Euphorbia griffithi* 'Fireglow', and *Iris laevigata* border the pond at Brook Cottage. By the late nineteenth century, the cottage garden style (opposite top) had been romanticized and had little to do with the subsistence gardens of the early cottagers. Primroses (opposite bottom) had long been favorite cottage flowers, and in the Victorian era began to attract the attention of plant breeders and specialty nurseries.

cottage style for a new generation of gardeners. In England, where the Thompson & Morgan seed company had been in business since 1855, there arose such influential nurseries—still operative today—as S. & N. Brackley (1890), the sweet-pea specialists; Blackmore & Langdon (1900), the delphinium, begonia, and primrose specialists; and Allwood Brothers Nursery (1911), the dianthus breeders, which introduced the first long-flowering pinks (*Dianthus × allwoodii*) to the horticultural world.

The English cottage garden was firmly established in the popular imagination.

These three plants were unknown to cottage gardens before the European discovery of the Americas. Left to right, they are the four o'clock (*Mirabilis jalapa*), woodland phlox (*Phlox divaricata*), and the sunflower (*Helianthus annuus*).

Cottage Gardening in the New World

John Josselyn's *New England's Rarities Discovered (etc.)*, published in England in 1672, revealed to the popular reader (in more than somewhat breathless terms) the botanical and zoological treasure that the early colonists had found in North and South America, a treasure that was to enrich beyond measure the cuisines and gardens of the world. Without the Americas, our kitchens would never have known string beans, chili peppers, chocolate, coffee, maize (which has yielded countless compounds of use in industry and cosmetics and which now feeds much of the world either directly, or indirectly as animal fodder), potatoes, pumpkins, summer squash (like zucchini), hard-shelled winter squash, or tomatoes. Without the Americas, our gardens would never have known four-o'clocks, marigolds (*Tagetes* spp.), monardas, nasturtiums, most penstemons, petunias, phloxes, evening primroses, scarlet runner beans, sunflowers, and countless ornamental trees and shrubs, such as catalpas and Apache plume (*Fallugia* spp.).

Yet even as North America exported its plants to the Old World, the Old World was sending its plants and garden conventions to the new, including its traditional weeds. (Before the colonists came, the New World did not know chickweed, ground ivy, mullein, nettles, or plantains.) By the late seventeenth century, colonists were growing in their geometric plots such imported plants as calendulas, carnations, catnip (by 1650), celandine, chamomile, white-flowered comfrey, coriander, dill, feverfew, single hollyhocks, honesty (said to be the first introduction), German iris, lavender cotton (santolina), the white lily (in America by 1630), musk mallows, pennyroyal, pinks, the opium poppy, rue, garden sage, garden sorrel, smallage, soapwort, stocks, tansy, sweet violets, and wallflowers. Most of the bushes and trees of the early colonial garden were European fruit varieties or single-flowered English roses, such as eglantine.

During the 1700s, the range of plants available to American gardeners steadily, if slowly, expanded, and not only because of the enthusiasm of English colonists. The Dutch and the French Huguenots (both of whom settled what is now New York's Manhattan and Flushing, respectively) were avid floriculturists, too. The first botanic garden in America was founded by John Bartram in Philadelphia in 1728. The first commercial nursery in America was opened for business around 1730 by Robert Prince on Long Island. (The Prince Nurseries continued to flourish into the mid-

1800s, eventually introducing Lombardy poplars to the United States and housing many of the plant discoveries of the explorers Lewis and Clark.) The first American greenhouse may have been built in Boston for one Andrew Faneuil, who died in 1737.

As a result of all this babble of plant lovers, it was in the eighteenth century that tomatoes began to appear in American gardens, as ornamentals. Lavender, originally thought too tender for the New World, was found adaptable. And among the vegetables that Thomas Jefferson grew at Monticello was a lettuce type called 'Tennis Ball', which is still available today from the Thomas Jefferson Center for Historic Plants.

In 1779, perhaps the first gardening book written by an American for Americans was published posthumously: *The Gardener's Kalendar* by Martha Logan of Charleston, South Carolina. Other important early American gardening books include *A Treatise on Gardening* (1793–1794), by a Gentleman of Virginia; *The Gentleman's and Gardener's Kalendar for the Middle States of North America* (1812), by Grant Thoburn, who opened New York City's first known seed store; and *The Young Gardener's Assistant* (1829) by Thomas Bridgeman. But to say these were American gardening books does not mean that they specialized in American plants. The European immigrants to North America had always tended to neglect native plants, preferring to import seeds, starts, and bulbs of many flowers and vegetables from Britain and the Continent. Andrew Jackson Downing, in *Rural Essays* (1854),

Despite the richness of native flora to be found in North America, most colonists imported the plants they grew. This little plot features cabbage, lettuce, and scarlet runner beans, all of which were brought to North America from Europe.

A re-creation of a New England cottage garden, this cheerful corner is filled with lilies, veronicas, wallflowers, and other traditional cottage flowers.

This lush kitchen garden, with its admirably straight rows, is very like the vegetable plots espoused by the British of Colonial America.

decried the practice, but as early as 1806 the trend was being viewed with alarm by none other than Bernard McMahon in *The American Gardener's Calendar*.

Bernard M'Mahon, or McMahon, was an Irish immigrant horticulturist living in Philadelphia. *The American Gardener's Calendar* was originally published in 1806 and went through eleven editions. The final edition, which appeared in the 1840s, bore the revised title *McMahon's American Gardener*. It runs to more than six hundred pages, and its subtitle makes it clear how comprehensive a treatment of American gardening practice it really is: "Adapted to the climate and seasons of the United States, containing a complete account of all the work necessary to be done in the kitchen-garden, fruit-garden, flower-garden, orchard, pleasure-ground, vineyard, nursery, greenhouse, out-house, and forcing-frames, for

every month in the year; with practical directions and a copious index."

While few home gardeners would have enjoyed the extensive nursery setup that McMahon describes—the book was written for professional horticulturists as well as for home gardeners—*McMahon's American Gardener* is a useful guide not only to the sorts of plants grown by Americans in the mid-nineteenth century but also to the (necessarily "organic") cultural practices used to produce them. And what of the poor tomato? The "tomato, or love apple," McMahon says, "is much cultivated for its fruit, in soups and sauces, to which it imparts an agreeable acid flavor; and is also stewed and dressed in various ways and very much admired." Despite these comments, he gives tomatoes only a little more space than Parkinson gave them in *Paradisi in Sole*, mentioning them only five times in the entire

volume and recommending no specific cultivars. He mentions potatoes even fewer times.

It is also interesting how little room McMahon gives to roses in his book. Although *McMahon's American Gardener* explains carefully how to bud, force, prune, and train flowering shrubs, including roses, and espouses wild roses and eglantine for hedges, it mentions Chinas, teas, and Bourbons only as classes and recommends no specific cultivars. To the modern reader, this may seem a curious omission for so comprehensive a volume. But according to Katharine Whiteside's *Antique Flowers*, rose breeding began at a fairly late date in North America—in Charleston, South Carolina, in the early 1800s—and perhaps early-nineteenth-century European varieties had not been disseminated widely enough for McMahon to deem them worthy of detailed discussion.

Some Important American Garden Plants by 1840

(From Bernard McMahon, *McMahon's American Gardener*)

Apples
Apricots
Artichokes, globe
Asparagus
Auriculas
Beans, kidney and Windsor
Beets (including "the Mangel Wurtzel, root of scarcity, or great German Beet")
Broccoli
Cabbages (such as "early Wakefield," "early York," and "sugar loaf")
Carnations
Carrots
Cauliflowers
Celery
Cherries

Chervil
Chives
Coriander
Cresses
Cucumbers
Currants
Eggplants (recently introduced)
Endive
Figs
Garlic
Geraniums ("or pelargoniums")
Gooseberries
Grapes (55 kinds, including wine and table types)
Hyacinths
Leeks
Lemons (under glass)

Lettuce
Melons
Mint
Mushrooms (in special beds of their own)
Mustard
Myrtles (under glass)
Nectarines
Okra (whose ground seeds he recommends as a coffee substitute)
Onions
Parsley (including parsley root)
Peaches
Pears
Peas
Peppers (still a novelty)

Pinks
Plums
Radishes
Ranunculuses
Rape
Raspberries
Rocambole
Salsify
Scorzonera
Shallots
Skirrets
Spinach
Squashes
Strawberries (including alpines)
Tansy
Tulips

PEPPERS

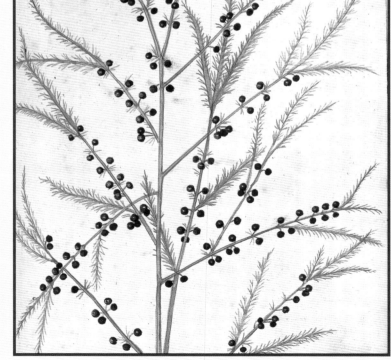

ASPARAGUS

After midcentury, the opening of the West and successive waves of Asian and European immigration introduced new vegetables, fruits, and flowers to North American gardens and popularized indigenous varieties that had been considered marginal. The health benefits of gardening for women, particularly flower gardening, also began to be preached, as by the Reverend Henry Ward Beecher in *A Plea for Health and Floriculture* (1859). And there seems to have begun a tussle, still going on today, between those who felt floriculture was serious gardening and those who felt it was not. This prompted Joseph Breck (1794–1873), the Boston seedsman and author of *The Young Florist, The Flower Garden* (which went through five editions between 1851 and 1866), and *The New Book of Flowers* (1866), to include within the latter an apologetics entitled "The Utility of Flowers: The Happy Influence of the Pursuit of Horticulture on the Mind of Man."

In 1863, the prominent New England horticulturist Fearing Burr, Jr., wrote and published *Field and Garden Vegetables of America.* It is not essentially a how-to book, but a comprehensive descriptive list of the named vegetable varieties available in the United States at that time. Burr compares varieties to one another and ranks them for dependability, earliness, flavor, texture, and suitability for table or fodder use; he notes different names for the same variety and denounces disease-prone, poor-keeping, or superseded cultivars. To give you some idea of the scope of this book, Burr lists nine kinds of chervil, twenty-two peppers, thirty-eight radishes, eighty-two turnips, one hundred forty-three peas, and eighteen

edible-podded peas. And finally, the poor tomato comes into its own. Burr lists more than thirty-five varieties, including a white. Most are medium- to cherry-size (Burr seems to consider the smaller varieties of little use in cooking), but several are as big as the modern beefsteaks: "Common Large Red," for many

During the Victorian era the belief took hold that gardening was a healthful pursuit (which it is), and women in particular cultivated flowers as if it were a competetive sport. Here, a tangle of columbines, foxgloves, chives, and lamium takes over a small plot.

years (according to Burr) almost the only kind of tomato known to most American gardeners, yielding fruits weighing from eight to twelve ounces (227 to 340g); and an improved selection "Giant," bearing huge irregular ribbed fruits that could reach four to six pounds (1.8 to 2.7kg) apiece.

Burr makes up for McMahon's neglect of the potato, too. He lists more than five dozen varieties, including six purplish blues, which he warns readers tend to be unpopular with the general public because of their outré coloring.

During the latter part of the nineteenth century, new plants from California and the southwestern United States, China, Japan, South America, and the Near East flooded U.S. markets. The American gardening craze was on, fed by improvements in rail transport, mail services, and shipping and storage technologies. During this period many mail-order nurseries, seed houses, and garden-related businesses were born, joining such old firms as the D. Landreth Seed Company (1784), purveyors to George Washington and Thomas Jefferson; Stark Brothers Nurseries & Orchards Company (1816); Breck's (1818); Comstock, Ferre, & Company (1820); and Crosman Seed Corporation (1838).

Improved shipping practices in the late nineteenth century meant that plants could more easily be imported or distributed from one region to another. This resulted in a gardening craze that possessed professional plant breeders and backyard gardeners alike.

Nineteenth- and Early-Twentieth-Century Gardening Firms That Have Survived to This Day

Allen Company (1885, now a berry specialists)

Allen, Sterling, and Lothrop (1911)

A.M. Leonard (1885, now a garden supplies house)

Beall Orchid Company (1906)

Brand Peony Farm (1868)

California Nursery Company (1865)

Cumberland Valley Nurseries (1902)

DeGiorgi Seed Company (1905)

D.V. Burrell Seed Growers Company (1899)

Farmer Seed and Nursery Company (1888)

Fennell's Orchid Jungle (1888)

Fischer Greenhouses (1888)

Gilbert H. Wild & Sons, Inc. (1885, now known for its daylilies and peonies)

Gurney Seed & Nursery Company (1866)

Harris Seeds (1879)

Hastings Nurseries (1889)

Hauser's Superior View Farm (1908)

Henry Field Seed & Nursery Company (1892)

Jackson & Perkins (1872)

J.L. Hudson, Seedsman (1911)

J.W. Jung Seed Company (1907)

Klehm Nursery (1852)

Krider Nurseries (1896, now a rose specialist)

Lafayette Home Nursery, Inc. (1887, now a specialist in prairie restoration plants)

Logee's Greenhouses (1892)

Long's Gardens (1905, iris specialist)

Ontario Seed Company (1899)

Oral Ledden & Sons (1904)

Park Seed Company (1868)

Piedmont Plant Company (1906)

Reasoner's (1881, now an orchid specialist)

R.H. Shumway's (1870)

Rod McLellan Company (1895, now an orchid specialist)

Roswell Seed Company (1900)

S. Scherer & Sons (1907)

Stokes Seed Company (1881)

Thomasville Nurseries (1898)

W. Atlee Burpee Company (1876)

Wedge Nursery (1878, now a lilac specialist)

William Tricker, Inc. (1895, now a water gardening specialist)

Wyatt-Quarles Seed Company (1881)

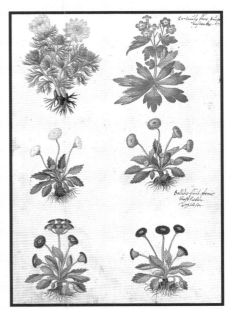

DAISIES AND RANUNCULUS

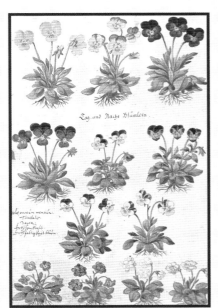

VIOLAS

Cottage gardens have a random, haphazard quality that lends itself to experimentation. As flowers pass out of bloom, you can plant untried specimens to fill the gaps, or you may wish to let nature take its course and allow plants to self-sow freely.

The look of chaos in the garden nearly redeems the rather grand house that dominates. A cultivated informality became all the rage after the Victorian passion for carpet bedding passed.

In England, the bedding plant craze, which had seen the destruction of so many lovely old gardens on both sides of the Atlantic, waxed and waned, to be replaced by an expanded and (to some extent) formalized cottage gardening style under the influence of designer Gertrude Jekyll and architect Edward Lutyens. U.S. gardeners, eager to stay in fashion, took note. But while Americans continued to take many of their cues in garden design from Europe, by this point the United States had a hoary gardening history of its own.

Even as improved transportation had made available to most gardeners a huge variety of ornamentals and food plants, improved national food-distributing technologies had deemphasized the subsistence role of the cottage plot, at least among suburban and city gardeners. Technological advances had hit the flower garden, too: home greenhouses were being marketed at unprecedented rates. In addition, a rising consciousness of the importance of the individual introduced to ordinary people in North America the idea that a garden could be the expression of one's distinct personality.

This straddling of old and new, informal and formal, old-fashioned and up-to-date is echoed in Helena Rutherford Ely's best-selling *A Woman's Hardy Garden*, published in 1903 by Macmillan, and its sequel, published two years later, *Another Hardy Garden Book*. Ely's books, written for the amateur with the smaller garden, include instructions in garden planning, insecticide use, and garden hardware and make detailed recommendations for all the best and easiest annuals, biennials, perennials, shrubs, trees, fruits, and vegetables.

Many cottage flowers are mentioned in the books, including roses. An advocate of the lavish use of annuals for cutting, Ely remarks, "We keep about 60 vases full in the house from late May until October." At the same time, she makes sure to remind the reader of her superb modern taste by asserting, "[Yet I] never allow more than two colours in the same room." The era of interior floral design had arrived.

War and Peace

After World War I, there came a phenomenal rise in the use of toxic pesticides and artificial fertilizers among farmers. Home gardeners followed suit, and before long, time-honored farming and gardening practices began to seem hopelessly outdated. During World War II, American citizens were encouraged to dig up their lawns and flower beds and raise vegetables, both to support the war effort and to supplement their rations. This further emphasized vegetable gardening as "serious" gardening. In the late 1940s and 1950s, when Americans could plant flower beds again without feeling guilty, the baby boom was on. More and more people began moving from the country to the cities and from the cities to the suburbs. Gardens began to be seen increasingly as "outdoor living rooms," extensions of the patio, more or less strictly controlled.

Centuries of farmland began to disappear under roads and parking lots. A few voices were heard in the shrinking wilderness—notably that of J.I. Rodale in the pages of *Organic Gardening* magazine, founded in 1942—but it was really not until the 1960s and 1970s that people began to question whether "modernity" was as promising as it had first appeared.

It was another nostalgic, simplicity-seeking, war-torn period for the United States. The civil rights movement, the assassination of President John F. Kennedy, and the Vietnam War protests were changing the way people thought about the role of civil authority in public life, including the intellectual authorities of patriotism and rationalism. Rachel Carson's *Silent Spring* (1961) alerted the general public to the previously largely ignored conservation movement. And a wave of romantic disaffection swept

through a new generation of young people. Terrified by the cold war and disillusioned by the urban solutions proposed by intellectuals of an earlier generation, hundreds of thousands sought solace in religious and rural utopianism. The back-to-the-land impulse and the drug culture combined to give gardening books old and new—particularly herb books—a ready market.

The elements of a revival of the cottage gardening mystique were in the air: a longing for rurality; a passion for self-sufficiency; an interest in flowers, herbs, fruits, and vegetables not only as food and medicine, but also as symbols of peace and tranquility; and a sense of history. The hippies of yesterday are the businesspeople, homeowners, plant nuts, and book-buyers of today. And a lot of them have found that cottage gardening speaks more closely to the ideals of their youth than any other horticultural style.

The aftermath of war brought the baby boom, smaller landholdings, and, inevitably, a nostalgia for what was imagined to have been simpler times. At Ashtree Cottage, a border of double violet cranesbill (*Geranium pratense* 'Plenum Violaceum'), 'Ballerina' rose, *Penstemon glabra*, and sweet William (*Dianthus barbatus*) recalls the gardens of cottages past.

41

CHAPTER TWO

PASSIONATE GARDEN PLANNING

"Search then the Ruling Passion: there, alone,

The wild are constant and the cunning known;

The fool consistent, and the false sincere...

This clue once found, unravels all the rest."

—ALEXANDER POPE

There are only a few principles you need bear in mind when planning your cottage garden, and they are:

- Too small a garden is a bore; too large a garden is a chore. Don't bite off more than you can chew. Start small; you can always add beds later as time permits.

- Site your planting beds to catch the best sunshine available. Some plants adapt well to part shade and others crave it, but most traditional cottage garden flowers and edibles need full sun.

- Before you plant anything, put in your paths, and make them wide. Four feet (1.2m) is the minimum. It may seem too wide in the beginning, but the first time you back your wheelbarrow over the emerging peony shoots you will wish you had given yourself more maneuvering room.

- Establish a regular soil-building program. Nothing contributes to the success of a garden more than spring and autumn applications of well-rotted compost (bagged mushroom compost works fine).

- Select and site your large specimen plants—trees, shrubs, and perennial vines—first, then build the rest of the garden around them. Make allowances for their mature sizes. In other words, don't do what I did, which was to plant a *Rosa alba* 'Semiplena' at the junction of two paths, where in three years it has swollen to the size of a baby elephant. And since of course I did not heed my own advice about path breadth, this specimen rose must be hacked back hourly so that it does not bring all comings and goings to a standstill.

- You don't need land to have a cottage garden: a perfectly luxurious cottage garden can be raised in half-barrels and other containers on a city patio or balcony. The crucial factor is light: as much sunlight as you can manage for the plants and as light a soil mix for the containers as possible. Make sure your containers have enough holes in the bottom to provide good drainage when you water, and do not—I repeat, do not—fill them with soil and plants until you have sited them, empty, first. It is also a good idea to check with your landlord before proceeding. Containers filled with soil and water tend to be heavy, and you don't want the charming Victorian facade of your brownstone to be crushed under the weight of your falling balcony.

Having said all this, I must add that there is no point in going to all the time, trouble, and expense to build a cottage garden unless you build the cottage garden you really want. This means, first and foremost, that your cottage garden must please *you*—not your designer, not your neighbors, not your garden club president, not Allan Lacey. But in order to create a cottage garden that perfectly reflects your deepest fantasies, you must know what those fantasies are.

How do you design a garden that from the first feels cottagey enough to satisfy you emotionally but permits expansion and embellish-

ment? You could take the Purely Intuitive Approach: buy a lot of different plants and arrange them in as many different ways as possible over many seasons until you hit on a design you like. This approach can lead to costly, time-consuming mistakes, and can cheat you of one of the central pleasures of

While lots of plants are rather finicky, you'll also find that there are plenty of flowers that thrive in most any conditions. Here are two such stars, spike speedwell (*Veronica spicata*) and salvia (*Salvia* × *superba*).

approach can lead to a planting with an air of rigidity rather than the spontaneity so important to the cottage garden feel.

A third method of designing the cottage garden (which you may have gathered is my favorite) is the Passionate Planning Approach, which makes intuition and intellect work together. It is based on the theory that of all the things I might want my cottage garden to look, feel, smell, taste, and sound like, some of these passions are more important than others. By figuring out at the start what I most want out of my cottage garden, I can invest my time, money, and space first where it will give me the most pleasure.

creativity, which is to translate a detailed vision into concrete reality.

Or you could take the Purely Analytical Approach: weigh the historical authenticity, height, color, bloom season, cultural requirements, size at maturity, availability, and cost of each cultivar considered and arrange your

selections on graph paper with all existing buildings, walkways, and plantings drawn to scale; then methodically set about reproducing the plan in three dimensions, removing unwanted plantings, walls, and walkways, augmenting the soil, laying down the irrigation system, and installing the cultivars. This

The Ruling Passion Exercise

The Ruling Passion Exercise is designed to help you find out what you most want out of your cottage garden, *before* you spend any money. It consists of making six lists as quickly as possible and compiling the results on a seventh sheet. You'll need at least an hour, probably several, to complete the exercise.

Label your first sheet "List No. 1: Uses"; your second sheet, "List No. 2: Sensory Pleasures"; your third sheet, "List No. 3: Emotional Pleasures"; your fourth sheet, "List No. 4: Garden Accoutrements"; your fifth sheet, "List No. 5: Prominent Plant Categories"; your sixth sheet, "List No. 6: Plant Musts"; and your seventh sheet, "List No. 7: Ruling Passions." Number sheets 1 through 6 along the left-hand side from 1 to 21, leaving a full line of space after each number. Number the seventh sheet from 1 to 6, leaving a line after each number. Now you're ready to begin your first list.

List No. 1:
The Uses of Your Cottage Garden

You begin by listing *all the uses* to which you might like to put your *ideal* cottage garden. Remember, we are talking ideals here; don't edit yourself for reasons of practicality. Pretend money, time, and fitness are no object. What do you want a cottage garden for? What do you want your cottage garden to do for you? How do you want it to enrich your physical, emotional, intellectual, or spiritual life? Here's my "Uses" list for your inspiration.

Please don't just copy it. Come up with your own ideas. The more personal you make this exercise, the better it will serve you.

List No. 1:
Uses for My Cottage Garden

1. a source of cut flowers
2. a source of fruit
3. a source of herbs
4. a source of vegetables
5. a private retreat from the cares of the workaday world
6. an ornamental setting for the house
7. a place to house my dianthus collection
8. something pretty to look at from the sunroom window
9. a means of getting exercise
10. a means of getting out my aggressions on those damn weeds
11. a place to make out with my beloved
12. a quiet place to read and think
13. a living history museum: medieval!
14. a classroom to teach adults how to garden
15. a place to pray
16. a means of boosting property value so that my landlord will take pity on me and not raise my rent too high
17. a project to take my mind off my problems
18. a source of gifts for my friends
19. a means of feeling more in control of my food supply
20. a means to show Mrs. Incarvillea next door that I'm a better gardener than she is
21. a place of abundance where I can feel prosperous

Now try the exercise for yourself. List as many uses as you can think of for your cottage garden, twenty-one if possible. You needn't finish the list at one sitting—take whatever time you require—but don't go on to the next list until you're done with this one.

This serene spot satisfies several garden cravings: potted herbs can be snipped for use; scented geraniums provide glorious fragrance; a rustic bench offers a chance to relax.

The Ruling Passion Exercise
Uses for My Cottage Garden

1. _____
2. _____
3. _____
4. _____
5. _____
6. _____
7. _____
8. _____
9. _____
10. _____
11. _____
12. _____
13. _____
14. _____
15. _____
16. _____
17. _____
18. _____
19. _____
20. _____
21. _____

If you get stuck making your garden "want" list, try making a "hate" list based on atrocities in friends' gardens. I love the surprise of pink in the garden here, but you may hate surprises. Be creative when thinking up uses for your garden: the setting opposite is a perfect subject for painting.

Getting Unstuck

If you found, performing the above exercise, that you couldn't think of anything you wanted to use your cottage garden for beyond the obvious, try to get ideas from books, childhood memory, others' gardens and your emotional reactions to them, catalogs (they're not called "wish books" for nothing), other gardeners, and magazines.

If you're still having a tough time, try making a "hate use" list instead of a "want use" list. Think of what you'd *hate* to have your cottage garden used for: "a dog run," for instance, or "one of those awful gardens where everything

is labeled in Latin." Then restate these hates as their opposites, or use them as clues to direct you to elements you would like. If you'd hate to see your garden turned into a run for your neighbors' pets, then, stated positively, what you must want is something like "privacy." If you don't want your garden to resemble an arboretum, then what you must want is something like "simplicity." You may find, as you develop your garden picture, that those qualities of privacy or simplicity turn up again and again in other areas, not just those areas relating to foreign pets and plant tags. They may be deep clues to what your heart really seeks from this project.

Finding Your Garden's Ruling Use

When you've finished your list of all the uses to which you'd like your cottage garden put, you must find the "Ruling Use" for your garden, the most important of the uses to which you'd like your garden put.

To do this, take the *top two* items on your "Uses" list. Ask yourself, "Assuming my ideal cottage garden could provide me with both No. 1 and No. 2, *which is more important to me?*" You are not doing without one element; you're simply ranking the two. Constantly remind yourself of this as you work through your lists: because most of us were taught that it's wicked

or impractical to expect to enjoy everything we want, we tend to think in terms of "either-or." *Circle the item that feels more important to you,* bearing in mind that you may have the one you didn't circle, too. You've simply voted the other use as more important.

In the sample list given above, my first two uses for my cottage garden were "1. a source of cut flowers" and "2. a source of fruit." If this were your list, you would ask yourself, "Assuming my ideal cottage garden could provide me with all the cut flowers I could wish for all season *and* an abundance of my favorite fruit, which use might be *more* important to me?" In my case, I felt that cut flowers took slight precedence over fresh fruit; so, knowing I could have both, I circled No. 1 as the more important. This made "a source of cut flowers"

the Ruling Use for my cottage garden, and "a source of fruit" a secondary use—important, but not as important.

Captains of industry take note: the first thing that tugs at you is usually the answer that most truly reflects your deepest fantasies for your garden. Remember, now is not the time or the place to be practical. This is a fantasy exercise. Practicalities come later.

Having ranked items No. 1 and No. 2 on your list, compare the one you circled—your Ruling Use so far—with the *third* item on your "Uses" list. Again, circle the more important of the two you are ranking. If you have chosen No. 3, then it becomes the new Ruling Use of your list, and you must continue by comparing it to No. 4, and so on down the list. What if you feel that the item you circled the first time is still your Ruling Use for your garden? Then circle nothing; simply move on to No. 4 and continue your comparisons. Continue working down the list in this way, comparing each Ruling Use to the next item, until you have come to the end.

If you were thorough in your list-making and honest in your comparisons, the *last item* circled on your "Uses" list is your true Ruling Use. This means that although all the other uses on your list are important, they are *secondary* uses. If your cottage garden fulfilled all the uses on your list except the Ruling Use, it would not feel worth it to you to put in all the time and effort and expense necessary to create and maintain it. Whereas if it fulfilled the Ruling Use but did not fulfill some of the other uses, you might be a bit disappointed but you could still feel satisfied with it.

Coping with Indecision

If you can't decide between two items as you work your way down a list, consider the following possibilities:

● You may be having trouble because you're trying to rank two items that are simply different ways of saying the same thing, as when trying to rank, say, "a spiritual retreat" and "a place to get in touch with my God."

● You may be having trouble because one item is a *general* category and the other a subset or specific example of it, as when trying to rank "a source of fresh flowers" and "a source of long-stemmed roses." In a case like this you need to decide which is more important to you, the general category ("fresh flowers") or the specific one alone ("long-stemmed roses").

Remember: by choosing one item you're not doing without the other; you're merely ranking them.

● You may be having trouble because you're trying to use reason rather than intuition to choose between the two items. Try this: place the hand you do not use for writing over your heart. Ask yourself, "If my heart could speak, which item would it choose?"

● You may be having trouble because you are trying to rush the exercise, are distracted, or are overtired, hungry, or ill. Try again later.

● You may be having trouble because you fear that if you get in touch with your true

heart's desires you will never be able to manifest them. Dream anyway. It is better to have loved and lost than never to have loved at all. And unless your Ruling Passion for your cottage garden is that it reproduce in miniature the gardens of Versailles, the dream you end up with will probably be practicable.

Logging Your Garden's Ruling Use

When you've determined your Ruling Use for List No. 1, write it on the top line of List No. 7 (the list you entitled "Ruling Passions" and numbered from 1 to 6). As you work through the other five lists—"Sensory Pleasures," "Emotional Pleasures," "Garden Accoutrements," "Prominent Plant Categories," and

"Plant Musts"—you'll transfer your Ruling Passion for each to the seventh list.

By the end of the exercise you will have compiled a list of all your Ruling Passions for building your cottage garden. They will serve as the essential guidelines for bringing the garden of your dreams into physical reality.

Composing Your Cottage Garden Picture

Ruling Passions for My Cottage Garden

1. Ruling Use: _____

_____

_____

2. Ruling Sensory Pleasure: _____

_____

_____

3. Ruling Emotional Pleasure: _____

_____

_____

4. Ruling Garden Accoutrement: _____

_____

_____

5. Ruling Plant Category: _____

_____

_____

6. Ruling Plant: _____

_____

_____

LIST NO. 2:
SENSORY PLEASURES

On this sheet, you will write down all the ways you want your garden to *look, smell, feel, taste, and sound*. What colors and shapes do you want to jump out at you when you walk into your garden? Do you like a lot of light or do you long for shade? Perhaps you want things to billow around you like gentle mist. Perhaps you want a look of spaciousness, or coziness, or grandeur. Do you want plantings that are low or high or in between? Do you need things very close to the house? Do you want to be able to take everything in at a glance from your porch? Do you want the sort of garden you can wander through with your trug and pluck ripe berries from the bough? And what about fragrance? Some gardeners don't think twice about it; for many of us it is one of the sine qua nons of gardening. What scents can you not live without?

Consider sound as well. If you are a deaf or hearing-impaired gardener this point may be irrelevant to you (unless you have frequent hearing visitors whom you wish to please), but many of us would feel lost without birdsong, the sound of tumbling water, the tinkle of wind chimes, and the rustle of foliage to accompany our weeding. And how do you want your garden to feel to your fingers, knees, and feet? I thought this an absurd question until a painful gravel path reminded me that I do a lot of weeding on my knees and I need my kneeling surfaces to be soft (I hate those knee-pad things).

When you have come up with at least twenty-one sensory pleasures you would like from your cottage garden, use the techniques described in the discussion of List No. 1 above to find the Ruling Sensory Pleasure of the list, and log it on List No. 7.

LIST NO. 3:
EMOTIONAL PLEASURES

We talk about a happy garden or a sad garden, but what we mean by this is that the garden makes us feel happy or sad. In this list, you note the ways you want your ideal cottage garden to *make you feel*: excited? peaceful? safe? refreshed? nurtured? Then find your Ruling Emotional Pleasure using the above techniques, and log it on List No. 7.

This is my kind of cottage garden. Here, everything is crammed together in little shocks of pleasure. A sundial focuses the lot.

LIST NO. 4:
GARDEN ACCOUTREMENTS

Garden accoutrements, or "dinghy fods" as my mother called them, include not only the wood, metal, stone, and plastic with which we build our gardens, but also the pits we dig and the mounds we build up to irritate the moles. Your Garden Accoutrements list might include mounts, allées; gazebos, ha-has, arbors, trellises, garden houses, greenhouses; patios, walks, fences, walls to plant things on or in; statuary, fountains, pools; topiary (counts as hardware because in my opinion topiaries are green rocks, not plants); urns, pots, and containers; doghouses, cathouses, dovecotes; birdcages, birdbaths, bird feeders; a plastic donkey with cart, a pink flamingo, windsock geese in a row.

List everything you can think of that you might like in your cottage garden. When it's time to find your Ruling Garden Accoutrement,

The herb feverfew (*Tanacetum parthenium*), left, carpets the ground in a glorious mass; willow plant supports stand at the ready for taller companions.

A bench, opposite, will enhance any cottage garden. This stunning example looks out over a garden filled with climbing roses, alliums, irises, peonies, and catmint.

ask yourself, "What on this list of dinghy fods could I not live without?" The answer gets logged on List No. 7.

LIST NO. 5:
PROMINENT PLANT CATEGORIES

You've found the Ruling Use for your cottage garden, its Ruling Sensory Pleasure, its Ruling Emotional Pleasure, and, Lord help us, its Ruling Garden Accoutrement. Now it's time to focus on the *plant categories* you want to form the backbone or theme of your garden.

The plant categories you list are entirely up to you. Some of you, being of tidy mind, will prefer to think in terms of botanical or horticultural categories, such as "the genus *Dianthus*" or "decorative grasses"; others, in terms of plant styles, such as "herbaceous perennials of sixteenth-century England"; and others, of specific plant uses, such as "flowers for cutting" and "medicinal herbs." Do stay away from naming specific cultivars at this point (that's for the next list). Now proceed as above, making your list of twenty-one, finding your Ruling Plant Category, and logging it on List No. 7.

LIST NO. 6: PLANT MUSTS

At last we come to List No. 6, where you daydream about the particular species or cultivars you can't live without. Here, again, plant books and catalogs will come in handy, but do not let practicality censor your list. If you live in Alaska and really, really, really want bananas in your garden, say so. When you've finished your list of Plant Musts, find and log the Ruling Plant, the one plant essential to your entire garden. Remember: *you may have all the others*. This is the one you call Queen.

COMPOSING YOUR GARDEN PICTURE

Having slogged through all this list-making, you should now have a pretty comprehensive picture of your ideal cottage garden. In fact, you may have such a comprehensive picture that it has satisfied your desire for a garden, and you can take up a less laborious hobby, like bungee-jumping. But some of you should find yourselves a-lather with excitement, ready to dive in and Do It. Here's the final picture I came up with from my List No. 7:

*Ruling Passions for
My Cottage Garden*

1. Ruling Use: a place of abundance where I can feel prosperous
2. Ruling Sensory Pleasure: intimacy; the look of a secret garden that the world has passed by
3. Ruling Emotional Pleasure: a place to give me hope

'**B**otany Bay' and 'Ballerina' roses clothe a pergola in this garden of soft pinks and purples. Color, scent, and structure should all be taken into account when planning a garden.

Below is passion in a pot: this delicious little cottage garden in a half-barrel features Swan River daisies (*Brachycome*), Marguerite daisies (*Argyrantheumum*), Helichrysum, blue lobelia (*Lobelia erinus*), and pansies (*Viola × wittrockiana*).

4. Ruling Garden Accoutrement: bird feeder
5. Ruling Plant Category: fruiting trees and shrubs small enough for easy picking but tall enough to feel abundant, say between four and eight feet (1.2 and 2.4m) tall
6. Ruling Plant: honeydew melons, with sweet tomatoes a very, very, very close second

Your list of Ruling Passions becomes your primary guide to the look, feel, and layout of your cottage garden. My final list told me I had to design a cottage garden that would provide me, at the very least, with an abundance of small fruiting trees and shrubs, particularly honeydew melons and sweet tomatoes, where a bird feeder was prominently located, and where I could feel an overall sense of privacy and secrecy. What does your final list tell you?

CHAPTER THREE

COLOR IN THE COTTAGE GARDEN

"The gardener must experiment [with color]
until the result excites him, then leave it alone."

—HENRY MITCHELL, *THE ESSENTIAL EARTHMAN*

Cottage gardens are invariably somewhat haphazard in their use of color, because cottage gardeners are forever trying out new plants. This means that they are forever moving old plants to new places, or to the compost heap, in order to free a happy patch of soil and light for the newcomers. All this trial and error can wreak havoc on the careful color plan. Another thing that can wreak havoc on the careful color plan is the garden planner's inability to imagine colors together. This is one of the things that makes me different from, say, Gertrude Jekyll or Vita Sackville-West—aside of course from the fact that they were talented garden designers and I am not. I do not have the mind of an artist, and they did. I have to see colors together physically to decide whether or not I like them.

I chose the plants I installed in Mother's Key West garden pretty much for utility and fragrance, not for color. After all, brilliant, flaming color is everywhere you turn in the subtropics. It wasn't until I moved to Santa Fe that I started considering color as a garden theme. It was the perfect milieu for the beginner: sand and brick tones everywhere you looked, with a tall, wide blue sky and a clarity of light that has drawn artists here for generations. The first things I planted were lavender bushes, primarily because I wanted to use the flowers in sachets but also because the cool gray-greens of their foliage and pale blue-purple of their flowers relieved the hot stare of my house's beige-washed walls. But if you had asked me my favorite color, I would not have said "lavender." I would have said "red." I only discovered how much I liked lavender by trial and error.

If some favorite colors emerged during your Ruling Passion Exercise (see chapter two), emphasize them when you go to make up your garden plan and shop for plants. But stay alert for surprises. When you're walking down the nursery aisle, snooping in your neighbor's garden, or leafing through a book of garden photographs, ask yourself, "How do these colors make me feel?" If you want your garden to make you feel peaceful, you might want to

Swathes of pink envelop this garden, courtesy of bellflowers (*Campanula latifolia*), salvia (*Salvia sclarea*), and stocks (*Matthiola* 'Bowles').

The soft gray foliage of rose campion (*Lychnis coronaria*), left, forms the perfect setting for its brilliant electric rose-purple flowers. No one in their right mind would dream of calling them red. Right, catalog writers?

Tulipa × 'Estella Rijnveld', below, is probably my favorite late-blooming red tulip. Here, it is mixed with white Parrot tulips and 'Fantasy' tulips.

emphasize blues, greens, cool rose, and very pale yellows. If you want your garden to lift your spirits, you might turn to reds, oranges, magentas, golds, and whites.

But you may find rose exciting, not restful. Some people do. It depends on the shade of rose, how much there is of it, and what else is planted around it. Give yourself permission to experiment. If you don't like a plant in one spot, you can always move it somewhere else. Or give it away. Or sell it in a yard sale and use the money to get something you really want. As my mother would say, "So who's counting?" As Henry Mitchell says in *The Essential Earthman*, "No color is 'safe' and no color is 'dangerous.' More gardens are rendered dull by timidity than are rendered vulgar by excessive daring. Be bold."

And remember that colors are very subjective. There are gardeners who insist that the wonderful old cottage plant *Lychnis coronaria* (rose campion or dusty miller) is red. It is not red. It has never been red. It is brilliant electric rose-purple. Yet I have seen it called red in catalogs. Are these people mad, these red-lychnis-ites? Not at all. To them, "red" is simply a broader category than it is for me. The fact that some of these chromatically broad-minded people are plant catalog writers, who know that "red" will sell faster than "electric rose-purple," is surely an utter coincidence.

So bear in mind that "red" in a catalog description can mean, in real life, that your coveted plant will end up blooming in anything from magenta through claret through purple through burgundy through oxblood

through what I call red—true Crayola crayon red—through scarlet through orange-red through orange. If it is an annual, it is a simple matter to pluck it from the soil and cast it upon the compost heap. It is not so easy to do this if the offending color is growing on a rhododendron.

Red tulips are essential to the best-dressed spring cottage garden, and there are dozens to choose from, I suppose. But if I could have only one red tulip, it would be the fabulous late-blooming red-and-white bicolor 'Estella Rijnveld'. 'Estella' grows twenty inches (51cm) tall, and it is of the Parrot class, so its petals are a bit nicked and twisted, like a parrot's feathers during grooming. For cutting, it is unmatched, and it naturalizes well and can be seen across the garden.

Everybody has a plant or two they would kill to grow well. Cardinal flower (*Lobelia cardinalis*), above, is mine. I adore its pure, saturated red, but in my climate I must be content with zinnias, above right.

I suppose the reddest native North American perennial I have ever seen is the cardinal flower, *Lobelia cardinalis*. I found it growing on the edge of our pond one summer when I was a teenager in Connecticut. The plant was skinny—around four feet (1.2m) tall and less than one foot (30cm) broad—and the blossoms, which were three-lipped above and two-lipped below, glowed in the marsh grass. In the irritating way of wildflowers, it had sprung up apparently from nowhere—we had never known it on our property before—and after that summer we never saw it again (it is said to be short-lived). If you can give cardinal flower the cool, moisture-retentive soil it needs, and are willing to replenish it from time to time

with seedlings or nursery starts, you can have it in your garden forever; it is hardy in Zones 2 through 9. Do not buy the white or salmon forms by mistake.

The Oscar for best overall red-flowered cottage garden annual has to go to those gorgeous scarlet zinnias that grow so well in the catalogs. Zinnia reds do not hurt the eyes; they are available from seed strains six to thirty-six inches (15 to 90cm) tall; and they ask only for good sun, regular moisture, and regular deadheading to charm your pants off all summer. The trouble is, not everybody can grow zinnias, scarlet or otherwise, because of a dreaded thing called powdery mildew, a whitish fungus that can turn any zinnia plant, seemingly

overnight, into a three-leaved single stalk with one overblown flower at the end of it. The open-pollinated, tetraploid strain 'State Fair' has done well for me most years. The years I cannot have zinnias, I grow red pompon dahlias instead. They never get mildew.

'Austrian Copper' is another easy grower. 'Austrian Copper' is the common name for *Rosa foetida* var. *bicolor*, a prickly, rangy ten-foot (3m) shrub with beautifully textured green leaves and single flowers in spring. The flowers are warm, matte orange-red on the upsides and a shocking cool yellow below, with prominent gold stamens and a surprisingly erotic scent. It is roughly a month from first flower to last, and as the petals fall they litter the grass beneath them with pieces of torn sun. I gather them for potpourris, because on drying they turn a true red. Mother's darling 'Tropicana' rose would bloom all summer, but my garden is too small for it; its saturated orange blooms would dominate everything around it as long as they showed themselves. 'Austrian Copper' does not last long enough to weary. Some call it blackspot-prone, but you couldn't prove it by me.

If you want an orange tulip worth crooning over, plant 'Orange Favorite' or 'Ballerina'. 'Orange Favorite' is a late-blooming tulip of the Parrot class, like 'Estella Rijnveld', growing twenty inches (51cm) tall and opening sweetly scented, twisty, soft orange petals marked soft green on their outsides and soft yellow at their bases. 'Ballerina' is a member of the slightly later-blooming Lily-flowered tulip clan. She is slender, with long, flowing, elegant lines and fragrant, pointed petals—very Persian. She is also (for once) properly described by the catalogs as "apricot-tangerine." At twenty-two inches (56cm) tall, she is like an aristocratic city heroine in a Jane Austen novel, while 'Orange Favorite' is her stouter, chummier, country kinswoman.

Asclepias tuberosa, the butterfly weed, is another glorious orange for the cottage garden, but it is not planted much out West; I can't think why. It is more common in the East. Butterfly weed has a big taproot that makes it

virtually impossible to transplant from starts. You need to raise it from seed, which is not difficult, and plant the seedlings where you want them to stay. The rich orange umbels are small but numerous, and they are almost shockingly beautiful when you see them for the first time. The plant is not at all weedy, though its stems are stout, and it is hardy over a wide range (Zones 3 through 10).

While the young plants are establishing themselves (and once they have established themselves, they are here to stay), you can grow around them or in front of them the stunning old English marigold, *Calendula officinalis*. You do not want just any calendula; you want the old seed-strain 'Radio'. Its clear, calm orange petals end in tiny bifurcations, which create a quilled effect, and it has none of the fancy-pants stippling with red-brown or washing with yellow that artsy modern calendulas possess. 'Radio' is simply orange. (I prefer calendulas to the *Tagetes* or New World marigolds because calendulas do well both in sun and shade, and *Tagetes* marigolds do not. I must admit, however, that my neighbor's border, which he fills every year with tall golden "African" marigolds, is as beautiful as anything can be.)

Among the most widely grown annuals in the world, marigolds (*Tagetes* spp.) yield not only orange and yellow but rust, pale cream, shrieking lemon, and bicolors. They are all desperately vulgar, and no cottage garden can be without them.

A Rainbow Border of Easy Annuals

You can follow the plan exactly, or feel free to substitute your favorite cottage flowers.

1. *'Crystal White' zinnia* (Zinnia angustifolia *'Crystal White'*)
2. *'Janie Deep Orange' French marigold* (Tagetes × patula *'Janie Deep Orange'*)
3. *California desert bluebell* (Phacelia campanularia)
4. *Dahlberg daisy* (Thymophylla tenuiloba)
5. *'Blue Splendor' Swan River daisy* (Brachycome iberidifolia *'Blue Splendor'*)
6. *'Empress of India' nasturtium* (Tropaeolum majus *'Empress of India'*)
7. *'Jubilee Gem' cornflower* (Centaurea cyanus *'Jubilee Gem'*)
8. *'Pacific Beauty Lemon' calendula* (Calendula officinalis *'Pacific Beauty Lemon'*)
9. *'Strawberry Fields' globe amaranth* (Gomphrena globosa *'Strawberry Fields'*)

10. *'Mont Blanc' lavatera* (Lavatera trimestris *'Mont Blanc'*)
11. *'King Size Salmon' larkspur* (Consolida regalis *'King Size Salmon'*)
12. *Chinese forget-me-not* (Cynoglossum amabile)
13. *Bells of Ireland* (Molucella laevis)
14. *'Zenith Series Goddess' zinnia* (Zinnia × elegans *'Zenith Series Goddess'*)
15. *'Rocket White' snapdragon* (Antirrhinum majus *'Rocket White'*)
16. *'Violet Queen' spider flower* (Cleome × hasslerana *'Violet Queen'*)
17. *'Grace Hybrid Red' godetia* (Clarkia amoena *'Grace Hybrid Red'*)
18. *Four o'clock* (Mirabilis jalapa)

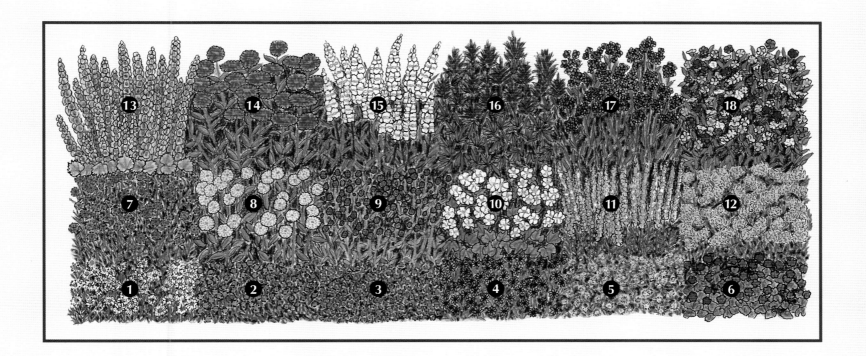

Of the breeding of narcissi there is no end, and I am afraid my favorite ones are not the yellow-petaled types, although the miniature yellow hoop petticoat daffodil (*Narcissus bulbocodium* 'Conspicuus') is adorable. Also, the scent of the pale yellow, orange-cupped *Tazetta* 'Scarlet Gem' is enough to knock your socks off. However, my favorite yellow-flowering bulb, the one I would have on a desert island if I could have no other, is the little-known Triumph tulip 'Bellona'. How can I convey to you

its perfection? It is not the tallest tulip, at only eighteen inches (45cm), nor does it have cunning fringes or arcane stippling. And though it can be forced indoors, it is at its best in big clumps outdoors in Zones 5 through 9, where it is quite hardy and remarkably persistent. I can only say that for purity of rich yellow color and sweetness of perfume, this tulip has no rival.

Aquilegia chrysantha, the North American native golden columbine, is a good perennial

Yellow and violet are opposites on the color wheel, and these complementary colors represent a favorite pairing of both painters and gardeners. Opposite, columbines in a clear yellow combine dramatically with violet-blue bellflowers.

While cottage gardens are traditionally a jumble of colors, the vogue for color themes sometimes asserts itself. The border above shows all the plant variety associated with the cottage style, but makes use of the yellow palette almost exclusively. Serene green foliage balances the sunny flowers, and judicious splashes of white and violet offer welcome visual surprises.

The fragrant yellow columbine *Aquilegia chrysantha*, left, and the sweetly scented 'Bellona' tulip, right, are two of the best yellows for the spring plot. A bouquet of either is a revelation.

to interplant with 'Bellona' as it will grow up and cover the leavings of the flowered bulbs. I had never heard of this southern native until I moved to Santa Fe, but it is the longest-blooming columbine in my garden, and softly perfumed to boot. Hardy from around Zones 3 through 8, it makes ethereal clumps that soon cover themselves with big, pale yellow, long-spurred blossoms even in semishade. It self-sows, too, and the seedlings are always welcome. There are improved selections from the species, notably 'Yellow Queen', but I am satisfied with what I have.

Except that I could do with many, many more plants of the sweet little annual

Dahlberg daisy (*Thymophylla tenuiloba*). Early one summer, in Santa Fe, I was wandering through one of my three favorite nurseries when I chanced upon a bank of pots grinning with numerous baby yellow daisies. By "baby" I mean just that: each flower head was no more than half an inch (12mm) wide, with yellow ray florets opening from a yellow central boss. The diminutive blooms rose from masses of dark green, much-divided, thread-like leaves on plants from six to twelve inches (15 to 30cm) high. I had never seen them before in my life.

Now Dahlberg daisies are not the sort of thing I usually go for. Their stems are too

Two delights: in yellow, wee Dahlberg daisies (*Thymophylla tenuiloba*) defy the curmudgeon all summer long; 'Big Daddy' hosta cools summer-fevered eyes in washes of blue-green.

short for cutting, and though the plants have a pleasant herb scent, we are not talking here of the perfumes of Araby. Yet the contrast between the precise gold of the little flowers and the amorphous dark green of the leaves is both charming and arresting; I never tire of it.

Dahlberg daisies are easy from seed, but I am lazy, so I bought a bunch of plants and put them in a sunny, well-drained patio half-barrel next to my front door. They filled out quickly, becoming a mass of gold.

It would be interesting to pair golden fleece with a little ground-fog of pink annual baby's-breath (*Gypsophila repens* 'Rosea') and dark violet sweet alyssum (*Lobularia maritima* 'Oriental Night'). But golden fleece alone is pleasure enough.

Now all the books say you must use twice as much green in your garden as you think necessary, and I am terribly afraid that they are right. Green, like water, is the universal solvent; tensions soak into it, and clashing colors harmonize through its influence. I do not like green flowers, except for jack-in-the-pulpit, mignonette, and some of the Viridiflora tulips, but there are many, many useful foliage greens. I eschew the yellow-greens, especially the gold-variegated greens. The last time I saw a gold and green together that I liked was on a croton in Key West, and I liked that croton only because its green was so dark and the gold so pure that only a dead person could be left cold by it. By contrast, most yellow-leaved sports of green-leaved flowers look chlorotic

to me, or as though herbicide had been spilled on them by mistake.

I am fond of dark greens, blue-greens, burgundy-greens, and silver-greens. Of these, it is the dark greens—so easy to come by elsewhere, what with your rhododendrons and boxes and privets and yews and hollies and hostas—that I long for most here in Santa Fe. That is why, next year, I am going to bite the bullet and put in some Oregon grape hollies (*Mahonia* spp.). There are numerous species and cultivars, but two of the most adaptable seem to be *Mahonia aquifolium*, a thornless West Coast native, and *Mahonia repens*, whose range extends to the Rocky Mountains.

Mahonia aquifolium has gorgeous, glossy, prickly, dark green leaves (which start out red-

This cottage-style herb garden, left, meanders along a deliberately overgrown path. The ferny foliage of bronze fennel combines beautifully with lavender, thyme, lady's mantle, and evening primrose. Opposite, the serene blue-green leaves of 'Halcyon' hosta provide a cooling accent to the hot-colored flowers beyond.

dish) on a low spreading bush about three feet (90cm) tall. Its little yellow spring flowers become blue-black berries beloved of birds. Creeping mahonia (*Mahonia repens*) is even shorter, one foot to three feet tall (30 to 90cm); its leaves, which start out bluish and turn purple-maroon in cold weather, are as rich a color as you could wish for. Its fragrant, spring-borne, dark yellow bellflowers become delicious frosted blue berries. *M. aquifolium* is classified hardy only to Zone 6, *M. repens* to Zone 5, but do not let that deter you from trying them in colder zones. Just make sure that they get well-drained soil in a site protected from wind.

If I could grow hostas, which I can't because they need more moisture than I can promise them in Santa Fe, I'd grow the blue-green ones, of which there are many: 'Aqua Velva', 'Betcher's Blue', 'Big Daddy', 'Blue Blazes', 'Blue Cadet', et cetera, et cetera. Instead I grow perennials of the *Dianthus* clan, particularly the Cheddar pinks (*Dianthus gratia-nopolitanus*). For example, 'Frost Fire', a hybrid *gratianopolis* four to six inches (10 to 15cm) tall, has particularly blue foliage (the "frost") and a bonus of double ruby blossoms (the "fire," I suppose). At two to four inches (5 to 10cm) tall, 'Blue Hills' is much shorter, making plants that resemble nothing so much as cute blue

hedgehogs. It flowers in what one catalog has described as "brilliant rose-magenta," which is putting it mildly.

And for really unusual foliage color, I plant bronze fennel, *Foeniculum vulgare* 'Purpurascens'. Effortless from seed, this hardy umbellifer is bronze-purple to bronze-green; the coloring is somewhat variable depending on the season and the genes of each seedling. I have selected in my garden for purpleness, roguing out the greens, so my tall 'Sensation' cosmos have a wall of dark mist against which to play their blushing games. When the fennels go to seed, either I allow the seeds to mature (the huge flat flower-umbels are the color of old gold) or

I whack the stems back to the ground, forcing another puff of dark smoke, which grows bigger daily until it manages to put up another flush of flowers, or until frost turns it to mush.

Now it is time for me to sing you the blues. One of the things I did right last year was to plant *Hyacinthus orientalis* 'Perle Brilliante', a rare nineteenth-century hyacinth from a specialist nursery, next door to a clutch of *Crocus* 'Blue Pearl', a not particularly rare crocus from a local garden center bin. Everything opened in April at more or less the same time, and imagine my surprise to find that 'Blue Pearl' and 'Perle Brillante' bloom in much the same miraculous blend of shimmering blues. Robin's-egg blue figures prominently in both, with tones of pale bluish lilac (particularly in the crocus). But from one hour to the next the hues shift.

Another thing I did right last year was to plant a plug of *Veronica liwanensis* between two flat stones at the front of a full sun border, and I mean baking full sun. Behind it I planted, among other things, three little buns of *Dianthus cruentus*, the bloody pink, which I had grown

There are scores and more to choose from when it comes to blue hyacinths. 'Dreadnought' hyacinth is a dusty purple-blue, with streaks of true blue running through the tiny florets.

A Perennial Bed in Pinks and Blues

Plant this design exactly, or use it to inspire your own blue and pink garden.

1. 'Her Majesty' pinks (Dianthus × plumarius 'Her Majesty')
2. 'Rose de Mai' pinks (Dianthus × plumarius 'Rose de Mai')
3. 'Dad's Favorite' pinks (Dianthus × plumarius 'Dad's Favorite')
4. 'Lady Granville' pinks (Dianthus × plumarius 'Lady Granville')
5. 'Berry Burst' pinks (Dianthus × plumarius 'Berry Burst')
6. 'Duchess of Westminster' pinks (Dianthus × plumarius 'Duchess of Westminster')
7. 'Lavender Lady' yarrow (Achillea 'Lavender Lady')
8. 'Wargrave' hardy marguerite (Anthemis tinctoria 'Wargrave')
9. 'Mousseline' autumn damask moss rose 'Mousseline': syn. 'Alfred de Dalmas'
10. 'Shibori' Japanese spirea (Spiraea japonica 'Shibori')
11. 'White Swan' coneflower (Echinacea purpurea 'White Swan')
12. Golden columbine (Aquilegia chrysantha 'Yellow Queen')
13. 'Journey's End' Oriental lily (Lilium × 'Journey's End')
14. 'David' summer phlox (Phlox paniculata)
15. 'Blue Giant' speedwell (Veronica longifolia 'Blue Giant')
16. 'Barnsley' tree mallow (Lavatera × thuringiaca 'Barnsley')
17. 'Black Knight' delphinium (Delphinium × 'Black Knight')
18. 'Sarah Bernhardt' peony (Paeonia 'Sarah Bernhardt')

from seed. By late autumn *D. cruentus* had not grown much bigger, but the little speedwell had tripled in size, and this spring it covered itself in tiny lipped flowers of a perfect, brilliant, true blue, a blue to make you gasp with delight, an actual piece of sky lying right there in front of you. It bloomed for fully two months. Eventually, the pinks became fearful that I might start an American Veronica Society, so they opened their rusty buds (the exact color of dried blood) and started screaming their tiny clustered heads off in the shrillest crimson red imaginable. I was in perfect heaven. The moral of this story is, blue and crimson go very well together in judicious doses.

I am always on the lookout for a flower that will combine the exquisite pale blue of the frost tender Cape leadwort (*Plumbago auriculata*) with frost-hardiness. Cape leadwort looks like a powder blue phlox, but don't tell me to grow *Phlox divaricata* because they aren't at all the same hue. *Iris reticulata* 'Natasha' comes close, blooming at three to four inches (7.5 to 10cm) high right after the snow crocuses. Darker are the phacelias. *Phacelia campanularia*, the California desert bluebell, grows six to sixteen inches (15 to 41cm) tall in dry sun, bearing in spring small, single, five-petaled, intensely gentian-blue flowers, prominently stamened in white. The more water you give this plant, the longer it will bloom. Its close and similarly neglected cousin is *Phacelia tanacetifolia*, the tansy-leaved scorpion flower or fiddleneck. The fiddleneck has finely cut, ferny leaves and very tiny flowers held in airy balls of blue. It earned its common name because the bloom stalks, as they open, uncurl like a fiddleneck fern (or a scorpion getting ready to strike). Now *P. tanacetifolia* is somewhat variable in its flower color—the books say the blossoms can veer into the mauve— but the ones I grew stayed blue until they went to seed.

Another indispensable true blue flower is the azure onion, *Allium caeruleum*, which sends up from its thin-leaved clumps in late May and early June sturdy stiff stems to two feet (60cm) high. Its flowers are held in a sphere of florets that open a pure, clear mid-blue. As they fade, which can take up to a month, they develop peacock blue tints; then the petals

Some catalog writers try to pass off *Phlox divaricata*, right, as true blue. Why, when it is perfectly lovely as it is? If you want deep blue, try the desert bluebell (*Phacelia campanularia*), far right. Its velvety petals are nearly cobalt. I have said far too little about the range of hue from lavender, lilac, and mauvey-blue to outright purple; that is, from *Nepeta* × *faasenii* 'Six Hills Giant', opposite left, through *Campanula glomerata*, opposite right.

fall and you are left with charming seedheads. Blue onions are cheap right now in the better bulb catalogs, so why aren't you growing dozens and dozens?

I do not wish to give you the impression that I dislike lavender, lilac, and mauvy-blue shades. I like them very much, as witness the fact that I planted roughly twenty feet (6m) of hardy English lavender, *Lavandula angustifolia*, in the hot harsh ell of my rented home. But I do not like them when they are pretending to be true blue.

I see I have nearly reached the end of my chapter, and there is so much to tell you yet. The deliciously fragrant Siberian catmint, *Nepeta sibirica*, has gorgeous darkish green leaves and nearly violet-blue flowers and is

horribly, horribly invasive. Confine it to a tub but *do* grow it.

Another thing you must grow is the cool little three- to six-foot (90cm to 1.8m) shrub bluebeard (*Caryopteris* × *clandonensis*). It has rather lancelike gray-green leaves and clusters of near-blue flowers in summer. This year I grew the cultivars 'Blue Mist' and 'Dark Knight' in back of a planting of annual rose malope and dwarf rose, pink, and white cosmos. Across the path from these lovelies I had put a deeply pink, reblooming 'Quatres Saisons' damask rose, and I don't mind telling you I nearly fell over I was so impressed with my good taste.

A word on navy blues and deep rich purple-violets: do not fear them. No matter that they disappear at a distance; interplant them

with bright yellow and rich rose. Plant lots of *Allium* × 'Purple Sensation', lots of *Campanula glomerata* 'Superba', lots of *Salvia* × 'Mainacht' ("May Night"), and lots of veronicas. For that matter, plant violets, *Viola odorata* and its fellows.

Do not fear creamy whites, either. *Campanula alliariifolia* 'Ivory Bells' has none of the purity of the white peach-leaved bellflower, but it blooms forever, is hardy as a stone, and, at eighteen inches (45cm), can be fit anywhere. Startle everybody by grouping it in front of *Knautia macedonica*, that wiry-stemmed, everblooming, oxblood-purple weed; the primrose-yellow *Scabiosa ochroleuca*; and *Penstemon barbatus* 'Prairie Fire'. Oxblood, primrose, hot scarlet, and cream—who said cottage gardening was for the fainthearted?

CHAPTER FOUR

FRAGRANCE IN THE COTTAGE GARDEN

"I know a little garden close,
Set thick with lily and red rose,
Where I would wander if I might
From dewy morn to dewy night."

—WILLIAM MORRIS (1867)

A cottage garden without fragrance is like a marriage without sex: respectable, but rather beside the point. It is difficult to overestimate the importance of fragrant plants to our ancestors. It was not until the middle of the nineteenth century that artificial fragrances became available for use in the perfume industry. For all of human history before that, if you wanted to make something smell good, you had to use a plant or animal derivative to do it.

There are gardeners for whom scent is irrelevant, but they are not usually cottage gardeners. Perfume of root, stem, leaf, flower, fruit, and seed is one of the great pleasures of the cottage plot, whether it is the scent of a 'Brandywine' tomato ripe from the vine or the scent of beebalm foliage drying for potpourri. Notice how many traditional cottage flowers are treasured for their perfume as much as for their beauty: hyacinth, narcissus, wallflower, and sweet-pea; rose, cottage pink, lavender, and carnation; honeysuckle, jasmine, lily, and moonvine—their sweet names lead you through the year from one pleasure to the next. These are sweets in which anybody can indulge, and there are countless more.

The first perfumes of my garden are exhaled by my little 'Snow Bunting' crocuses, offspring of *Crocus chrysantha*, gold on their insides, white-streaked purple on their out-

The scentless cottage garden is practically a contradiction in terms. Whether it is the perfume of ripening strawberries, above right, or the heady scent along a lavender-bordered path, right, the cottage garden is a feast for the nose.

sides. Hard upon their blooming come my Reticulata irises, which resemble nothing so much as the punctuation marks of some unguessably glorious language. The ruddy purple *Iris × reticulata* 'J.S. Dijt' is the one to grow; it smells just like grape lollipops. So do the grape hyacinths (*Muscari* spp.) that start waving their wands around the same time. All of them are pretty, even *Muscari armeniacum* 'Blue Spike', whose little florets possess double the petals. I also grow the white Italian grape hyacinth, *Muscari botryoides* 'Album'. Hardy in Zones 2 through 8, it blooms in April and is just as fragrant as its blue relatives. There is a man in my neighborhood who lines his narrow brick walkway with grape hyacinths, and I do not know which is the more beautiful, the masses of slender flower spikes or the dense shiny green of the grass that follows them.

I do not scorn the big hyacinths, either, which makes no practical sense; their bloom time is rather brief and they make lousy cut flowers (their stems are really much too short). I am particularly interested in old cultivars, and I have collected several: the intensely blue-purple, double-flowered *Hyacinthus orientalis* 'General Kohler' (introduced to commerce in 1878); the single-flowered 'Distinction', leaner in shape than some, but of an impossible dark maroon (introduced in 1880, the year my Grandma Mid was born); pure white 'L'Innocence' (1863); and of course the near-blue 'Perle Brilliante' (1895). But any bag of mixed-color hyacinths will do. Some discounted bulbs I planted in 1992 still come up every year, as cheerful as dogs; and how I look forward to their noses poking up out of the soil.

People don't often think of tulips as being perfumed, but of course some are, particularly the Single Early types, which include the oldest cultivars still seen in gardens; the Double Earlies; and a few of the Triumph types, which are hybrids of the Single Earlies and various late-flowering cultivars. Yellows and oranges tend to be the most highly scented. The fragrance of tulips is hard to describe: refreshing, yet slightly waxy, a bit like the red lipstick my mother wore in the 1950s, with a middle note of sun-warmed sugar. I have already mentioned the scented eighteen-inch (45cm) -tall yellow Triumph tulip 'Bellona', the Parrot tulip 'Orange Favorite', and the Lily-Flowered tulip 'Ballerina'. But do you know the scented species tulips, such as the tiny, clear yellow and bronze Iberian tulip, *Tulipa celsiana* 'Persica', or *Tulipa sylvestris*, the little yellow and green woodland tulip? Both have a lovely fragrance and naturalize easily in a dry summer locale in full sun.

My favorite fragrant narcissus is drawn from the Tazetta or bunch-flowering group. It is 'Scarlet Gem', which was introduced around 1910. Every spring it bears golden yellow petals and flat, frilly red-orange cups on fourteen-inch (35.5cm) tall stems. Hardy in Zones 5 through 9, 'Scarlet Gem' is quite upright in habit, blooming for me rather early in the season. Its fragrance is a peculiarly masculine combination of wine, honey, and musk. Since it is getting scarce in the catalogs, I encourage you to demand it from your bulb supplier. 'Cragford' and 'Geranium' are lovely Tazettas, but they should not be permitted to supplant 'Scarlet Gem'.

I am aware, by the way, that the very late-blooming Poeticus group of narcissi is so beautiful and sweetly scented as to beggar description. But the poet's narcissus I knew as a child, with its perfect, snow white petals and

You must get down on hands and knees to enjoy the scent of the grape hyacinth (*Muscari* spp.), but it is worth the effort. One species, the rare *Muscari muscarimi*, smells like musk perfume.

Dangerous, glorious, sexy wallflower, now known as *Erysimum cheiri*, thrives in the cold weather of spring and autumn. Wallflowers are the Aphrodite of the cabbage family. Opposite, the gentle perfume of apple blossoms wafts over this spring garden; grape hyacinths and tulips add their fragrance to the mix. Search through the catalogs and nurseries to find tulips of sweet scent—orange- and yellow-flowered varieties most often carry fragrance.

tiny, red-rimmed yellow cup, does not take well to my Santa Fe climate; I am not sure why. All the bulbs I have ever planted come up with yellowish white, rather than pure white, petals, and only a mild perfume.

Weeks before the last of the tulips are reaching their peaks, the wallflowers (*Erysimum cheiri*, once *Cheiranthus cheiri*) are blooming in thick clusters of gold, yellow, bronze, red, plum, or white. These ancient garden plants possess cross-shaped blossoms that remind you they belong to the crucifer family, like

mustard and broccoli. Wallflowers' long, narrow leaves and stout stems are very like those of stocks, but their leaves are a stiff, dark, lustrous green rather than grayish. The reds and golds in particular breathe a sweet warm scent reminiscent of perfumed glove leather, or the perfume from those big, old-fashioned, black-faced yellow pansies you used to be able to buy in flats from the nurseries.

With age (wallflowers are perennials commonly grown as annuals or biennials) the plants become quite woody. Grown from seed started

indoors in February, then transplanted in April to a sunny, well-drained, neutral to alkaline spot, these beauties are completely hardy for me in my Zone 6a mountain garden; in fact, they are evergreen. Older kinds, such as 'Cloth of Gold', blossom profusely the following spring and every spring thereafter. Newer bedding strains will flower the first year.

Wallflowers appear to be native to Mediterranean Europe, where they often used to be found colonizing old walls, quarries, and sea cliffs. They are among an important handful of cottage garden plants that were once called "gillyflowers," from the Latin *caryophyllus*, the medieval scholar's name for the clove-spice tree. Another gillyflower was the dame's rocket or sweet rocket, *Hesperis matronalis*: early names for it were "rogue's gillyflower" or "Queen's gillyflower" (perhaps the rogues gave bouquets of them to queens).

Hesperis matronalis has only recently become widely available in North American nurseries. Although double-flowered forms of it, now virtually extinct, once brought it into vogue among flower breeders, dame's rocket has always been essentially a country flower—a big, lush, late-spring-to-early-summer biennial, occasionally perennial, that provides

astonishing height and six dependable weeks of blossom at a time when most of us are still thinking small and bulbous. It gets to be two to four feet (60cm to 1.2m) tall, with rich, green, long, pointed oval leaves tinged purplish in cold weather, and it will bloom even in shade, though it prefers sun. In my mountains, it flowers as early as late April and as late as late June, its four-petaled cruciform blossoms showing purple, lilac, or white. It is at night that dame's rocket releases its soft sweet fragrance, a habit that earned it the German nickname of "night violet."

Dame's rocket is surprisingly drought tolerant once established, utterly pest-free, and, though it self-sows amiably (there are always

little clumps of it springing up here and there), it never becomes a pest. I plant the roots in banks against my north-facing wall (all white ones this year), where they billow into blossom for a month at least. If you cut them way back when the flowers start going to seed, the plants will bloom again for you, albeit more sparely and a trifle closer to the ground.

The fragrance of the sweet-pea, *Lathyrus odoratus*, is another spring cottage garden essential. The origins of the sweet-pea are unknown, though wild forms have been found both in Cyprus and in Sicily, and it was a Sicilian monk, Franciscus Cupani, who first described the plants in print in 1697. They bore maroon and deep purple blossoms, much

The sweet purple florets of dame's rocket keep company with heart's ease (*Viola* × *wittrockiana*), sage (*Salvia* spp.), pot marigolds (*Calendula* spp.), and nasturtiums (*Tropaeolum majus*).

Sweet-peas (*Lathyrus odoratus*) like heavy soils and can take heat if their roots are cool and shaded. However, you must keep them picked or they will stop flowering.

smaller than those of the modern sweet-pea but far more fragrant. The first sweet-peas with frilled petals appeared as spontaneous mutations in several different places, including the Northamptonshire garden of the Countess Spencer and, slightly later, the garden of W. J. Unwin, a Cambridge grocer. This is the form of sweet-pea with which we are most familiar today.

Sweet-peas, like pinks, have an undeserved reputation for being hard to grow. It is true that they prefer cool weather and are subject to the same sorts of diseases and insects that plague English shelling peas and string beans. But that does not stop you from growing peas and beans, does it? I start my plants indoors in peat pots at about the time the farmers in my area are planting edible English peas outdoors.

About a month before our final frost-free date, I plant my sweet-peas outdoors in a well-dug bed enriched with low-nitrogen, high-phosphorus fertilizer, like a commercial 5-10-5 (as legumes, sweet-peas take their own nitrogen from the air and do not need a lot of additional nitrogen to thrive). If you plant your seedlings too early, and the frost turns their leaf edges white, fear not; you may lose a few seedlings, but most of them will simply sulk until the soil warms up enough for them to start active growth. Once active growth begins, mulch the plants well to keep the soil around their roots cool, and train them to their trellis as they grow.

All this attention should provide you with enough bouquets to perfume a seraglio. In *The Fragrant Path*, Louise Beebe Wilder suggests

framing sweet-pea nosegays with rose geranium leaves. Sweet-peas are also nice in bouquets with *Anthemis tinctoria* 'Moonlight' and 'Pale Moon', the softer cultivars of ox-eye chamomile; white dame's rocket (*Hesperis matronalis* 'Alba'); single-flowered columbines (*Aquilegia* spp.); stocks (*Matthiola incana*), whose somewhat earthy fragrance they sweeten; the blue-flowered onion (*Allium caeruleum*); and Chinese delphiniums (*Delphinium* × *belladonna*).

By the time my sweet-peas are clambering freely, my peony is blooming. It is not any of the fancy kinds, because the fancy kinds are too expensive for me, and I do not want anything in my garden that I am afraid of. It is plain old 'Festiva Maxima', introduced to commerce from France in 1851. The plants stand nearly three feet (90cm) tall, with sturdy, dark

Left to right, Rosa 'Boule de Neige', 'Buff Beauty', and 'Celeste', three tough old dames whose perfume will knock your socks off. They are not ever-blooming, but who is?

green leaves and big, petal-crammed, white flowers flecked variably with red. Its scent is sweet and sexy. My mother grew this flower, and when I was a child I used to dare myself to smell it when it was in bloom, because the ants loved the nectar and would swarm everywhere across its petals. Once you get into peonies seriously it is difficult to stop, so I have not gotten very far into them; but someday my resolve will crack. By the way, the majority of peonies on the market today are not strongly perfumed, which is an insanity. If I dared, I would collect all the heirloom scented types I could lay my hands on, including the silver-pink double 'Mons Jules Elie' (introduced in 1888); the pink, yellow, and white anemone-flowered 'Petite Renee' (1899); and, of course, 'Sarah Bernhardt' (1906), rather weak-stemmed but worth it for its exquisite, double, shell pink blossoms.

This brings us to roses. For years I thought I was death to roses and did not try to grow any. When I moved to Santa Fe, I could resist

no longer, so I planted a bush of the hybrid tea rose 'Tiffany' against the rosy beige plaster of my hottest south-facing wall. I chose it for its fragrance, and only after it had given me three years of glorious blossom did I find out it is considered a blackspot-hound and difficult to grow well. My success went to my head, and as my mother would have said it, I "went to town." I planted *Rosa foetida* 'Austrian Copper', which I told you about in chapter three; David Austin English roses; old Hybrid Perpetuals; a Gallica; and the red climber 'Don Juan'. All died except for 'Austrian Copper', which could survive nuclear attack; a chlorotic but bloom-heavy Damask, *Rosa* × *damascena* 'Quatres Saisons'; 'William Shakespeare', an Austin that continues to struggle in a back bed increasingly overrun by a cunning little horehound plant my friend Nancy gave me seeds for; and the White Rose of York, *Rosa alba* 'Semiplena'. And, of course, 'Tiffany'.

If I had it to do over again, I would have planted the whole yard with Alba roses and

Some Roses of Strong Perfume

The following roses will provide the cottage gardener with rich scent both in the vase and in moist or dry potpourri. All cultivars listed below bloom once annually, usually in late spring or early summer; repeat-blooming cultivars are noted as such in the text. Cultivars suited to growing in containers or small gardens are indicated by an asterisk in the height/spread section.

Name and Description	Height/Spread
R. × Alba 'Semiplena' (White Rose of York): tough; semidouble white; ancient	6 × 6
R. × Centifolia 'Muscosa': syn. 'Common Moss', 'Old Moss'; toothed leaves, furry stems and buds, long-bloomer; rich pink	5 × 4
R. × Damascena 'Bifera': syn. 'Quatres Saisons'; the Autumn Damask; loose, clear pink double flowers; blooms spring and autumn; ancient	5 × 4
R. × Damascena 'Trigintipetala': one source of rose attar; rich rose-pink; ancient	6 × 5
R. Gallica 'Officinalis': syn. Apothecary's Rose, Red Rose of Lancaster; semidouble crimson; ancient, in European gardens by at least 1430	*4 × 3
R. Rubiginosa: syn. R. eglanteria; Eglantine, Sweetbriar; grown for its foliage, which is apple-scented in moist weather; thorny; pink single flowers; ancient	12 × 8
R. Rugosa: Rugosa Rose, Japanese Rose; very prickly, very vigorous, hardy, wrinkled leaves, single dark rose-red; excellent salt tolerance; ancient	6 × 6
'Angel Face': Floribunda; pinkish-lilac, repeat-flowering, very sweet scent; 1968	*4 × 3
'Belle De Crecy': Gallica; nearly thornless, pink to violet flowers; since 1848	*4 × 3
'Blanc Double De Coubert'; very hardy; repeater; gorgeous snow white	5 × 4
'Boule De Neige': Bourbon; upright; repeat bloomer; cupped white flowers; 1867	5 × 3
'Buff Beauty': Hybrid Musk; vigorous, floriferous, informal pale yellow flowers in clusters; fade to buff; 1939	6 × 6
'Celeste': syn. 'Celestial'. Alba, rounded bush; pale pink; late 1700s	6 × 6 or more
'Double Delight': Hybrid Tea; ivory edged dark rose-red; rich old rose scent; 1977	*4 × 4
'Felicite Parmentier': Alba, bushy; rounded white pinkish white flowers; 1834	5 × 5 or more
'Jacques Cartier': Portland-China; repeat-flowering, pale pink with button eye	*4 × 3
'Louise Odier': Bourbon; vigorous, bushy; lilac-pink blossoms; reblooming; 1851	6 × 5
'Madame Hardy': Damask; pure white double flowers with green eye; 1832	6 × 5
'Madame Isaac Pereire': Bourbon; untidy; rich rose-pink flowers; reblooms; 1881	7 × 5
'Marie Louise': Damask; Lax arching; large flat mauve-pink; since 1813	5 × 4
'Mary Rose': Austin; long bloomer; vigorous, rich pink fading to pale pink; 1983	4 × 4
'Mousseline': syn. 'Alfred de Dalmas'; Autumn Damask Moss; lightly mossed, repeat-flowering, palest pink lax double blossoms; 1855	*3 × 2
'Parfum De L'hay': Hybrid Rugosa; vigorous, rebloomer; large cherry-red flowers	5 × 4
'Paul Neyron': Hybrid Perpetual; few thorns; long-blooming; huge rose-pink flowers	6 × 5
'Petite De Hollande': syn. 'Pompon des Dames'; free-flowering miniature Cabbage Rose; pink; since late 1700s	*4 × 3
'Reine Des Violettes': Hybrid Perpetual; nearly thornless; bears carmine or cerise flowers fading to violet shading; needs good soil; 1860	6 × 5
'Rose De Meaux': syn. R. centifolia 'Pomponia'; adorable miniature with small leaves and pink pompom flowers; by 1789	*2 × 2
'Roseraie De L'hay': Hybrid Rugosa; big semidouble purple-crimson; repeater; 1901	6 × 5
'Salet': Autumn Damask Moss; repeater; furry green buds, rich old rose blooms; 1854	5 × 4
'Zephyrine Drouhin': Bourbon; nearly thornless, very vigorous, very long-blooming, with large bright rose-pink flowers; 1868	$8^{1}/_{2}$ × 8

David Austin, or English, roses are modern roses bred for old rose traits, including intense fragrance. Here, 'Albertine' and 'Alexander Girault' clamber up a sturdy support.

said to hell with it. 'Semiplena' is a glory: drought tolerant, insect tolerant, alkali tolerant, heat tolerant, cold tolerant, even dog pee tolerant. This is my third year with it, and it has grown seven feet (2.1m) tall by seven feet wide of heartbreaking blue-green foliage, bursting in late spring with exquisitely pure white, joyously perfumed, single to semidou-

ble roses, each with its own prominent central boss of spun gold. By autumn, these roses have been replaced with big orange-red hips that are themselves so decorative they are worth the price of the plant. So what if 'Semiplena' blooms only once a year? So do lilacs. So do all those bloody little saxifrages everybody goes on and on about.

By this time my pinks (*Dianthus* spp.) have gotten well under sail. We always think we know what we mean by "pink": a small, grassy-leaved spring flower descended from the wild *D. plumarius*, offering five or more jagged-edged petals, clove perfume, and sometimes an edging or central eye zone of a contrasting color. In fact, the *Dianthus* clan is so promiscuous that any given pink is likely to be a mongrel, offspring not only of *D. plumarius*, but also of the carnation (*D. caryophyllus*), the Cheddar pink (*D. gratianopolitanus*), and many others. For the cottage gardener, however, pedigree doesn't matter as much as performance, so let me just say that I have never met a scented pink I didn't like.

The pinks most commonly offered for sale in North American nurseries are usually seed strains, such as 'Spring Beauty'. I have found some highly scented individuals among them. But you can always count on the fragrance of some of the lesser-known species pinks. The first to greet the New Year in my garden is always *Dianthus arenarius*, the little sand pink, with its blue-green mats of foliage and its deeply fringed, single, starry white blossoms, beginning in late April. The sand pink, which can get as tall as eleven inches (28cm) in flower, grows as well on well-drained clay loam as it does on sand, so don't let the name fool you; this is not one of those fussy alpines. Nor is *Dianthus squarrosus*, an eight-inch (20cm)-tall, sweet-scented Ukrainian with grass green leaves and deeply cut white blossoms. Both of these species pinks are rock-hardy, to Zone 3 if given very good drainage.

The lacy single flowers of *Dianthus alpinus* 'Allwoodii' offer a subtle sweet scent.

A bit less hardy perhaps, but still enormously reliable, is the Cheddar pink, *D. gratianopolitanus*. The Cheddar pink was called the "matted pink" in Elizabethan times, and this perfectly describes its habit: a carpet of blue-green needles hugging the stony ground it loves, giving rise in late spring and early summer to fringed pink fragrant single blooms that appear rather large for the foliage. The Cheddar pinks (and the Cheddar cheese, for that matter) are so named because they are native to the rocky Cheddar Gorge of Somerset, England; and the pinks (not the cheese) have been crossed with other alpine species to produce many low-growing cultivars ideal for softening borders, walls, and paving stones. Two excessively cute mutant Cheddars that do well for me are 'Spotty', sporting single, rose-red blossoms spotted white, and 'Tiny Rubies,'

a rose-red so double that it looks like an infinitesimal carnation. 'Tiny Rubies' has the charming distinction of being one of the best dianthuses for candying.

My favorite modern pinks are 'Her Majesty' and 'Aqua'. They are both fully double (thanks to what I suspect is their hidden carnation blood) and snow white, with a delicious perfume that keeps pouring out of them, particularly at night. The flowers are misshapen—their petals split the calyx and spill out like a courtesan's lace from her bodice—and the weak stems flop terribly. I have flopped terribly for years, so this does not bother me.

If you can grow only one pink, may I suggest the heirloom 'Rose de Mai'? Introduced to gardens around 1820, this vigorous plant, ten to sixteen inches (25 to 41cm) tall at maturity,

sports blue-green foliage and pale creamy mauve double to semidouble flowers, sometimes stippled maroon at center. The petals are not very "pinked," or jagged-edged. 'Rose de Mai' is certainly hardy to the warmer areas of Zone 4, but it is equally at home in Zones 7 to 9. Needless to say, it is wonderful for cutting and can rebloom in cool climates.

Since their blue to gray-green foliage remains attractive long after they have bloomed, cottage pinks make good plants for the front of a border. Just bear in mind that all dianthuses require good drainage, particularly in winter, and that they tend to do better in neutral to alkaline soils (add lime if you live in a low-pH area). Also remeber that dianthuses in general resent heavy organic mulches—instead you'll want to use a mulch of stone, gravel, or sand.

The gray-green foliage of 'Little Jock' dianthus sets off its heavily scented semidouble blooms.

Some Strongly Scented Cottage Pinks

'Amaranth'	Large single deep pink, maroon eye, to 12" (30cm)	Zones 4–9
'Aqua'	Pure white flowers, blue-green foliage to 12" (30cm)	Zones 5–9
'Baby Blanket' ('Far Cry')	Single pink to 6" (15cm), prolific, all summer if deadheaded	Zones 5–9
'Bath's Pink'	Heat-loving 10" (25cm) single, eye, blue-green foliage	Zones 4–9
'Berry Burst'	10–12" (25–30cm) single bright pink-raspberry, grayish foliage	Zones 4–9
'Dad's Favourite'	Late 18th century, white, edged ruby, purple eyed, 10" (25cm)	Zones 4–9
'Dottie'	Matted to 5" (13cm), adorable maroon and white singles	Zones 4–9
'Duchess of Westminster'	12" (30cm), pink, baby peony–like blooms	Zones 5–9
'Emile Pare'	Semidouble deep pink trusses, long bloom	Zones 5–9
'Essex Witch'	Semidouble rosy blooms, gray mats, to 8" (20cm)	Zones 5–9
'Fair Folly'	17th century, strawberry on white, 12" (30cm), floriferous	Zones 5–9
'Fenbow's Nutmeg Clove'	Deep red, 20–24" (51–60cm), bluish green foliage	Zones 6–9
'Gloriosa'	Pink, crimson eyed, 12" (30cm), greyish foliage, long bloomer	Zones 5–9
'Her Majesty'	By 1891, pure white, floriferous, 10–12" (25–30cm)	Zones 5–9
'Inchmery'	18th century, pale pink, floriferous, grayish foliage, 15" (38cm)	Zones 4–9
'Itsaul White'	Pure white, fringed, heat tolerant, 8–10" (20–25cm)	Zones 4–9
'Kaleidoscope' ('Kiwi Magic')	8–10" (20–25cm), white, red-purple eye, very prolific bloomer	Zones 4–9
'La Bourboule'	La Bourbrille, pale pink, mats, gray foliage	Zones 3–8
'Lady Granville' ('Lady Glanville')	1840, white with burgundy edge, eye, to 10" (25cm)	Zones 4–9
'Little Jock'	Semidouble pink with red eye, grayish foliage to 4" (10cm)	Zones 5–9
'London Delight'	Pale pink, reddish eye, edging; scent can be variable	Zones 5–9
'Mike's Mom's Cinnamon Pink'	Heirloom, pink with darker markings, blue foliage	Zones 4–9
'Mrs. Holt'	Clear pink single, neat buns to 6" (15cm)	Zones 4–9
'Mrs. Sinkins'	19th century, white, often bursts calyx, famous, to 10" (25cm)	Zones 5–9
'Musgrave's Pink' ('Charles Musgrave')	18th century, single white, green eye, enchanting	Zones 5–9
'Nova'	5" (13cm); tall single red, slightly darker eye, grayish foliage	Zones 5–9
'Old Spice'	Fringed salmon pink, long bloomer, 10–12" (25–30cm)	Zones 4–9
'Painted Lady'	Pale pink splashed deep red, bluish foliage, 8–12" (20–30cm)	Zones 5–9
'Pike's Pink'	Adorable pink, compact, to 4"–12" (10–30cm)	Zones 5–8
'Prairie Pink'	Shocking pink, sturdy upright plants to 24" (60cm)	Zones 4–9
'Queen of Sheba'	17th century, single ivory white etched magenta	Zones 4–9
'Raspberry Tart'	Semidouble, raspberry with maroon eye, 8–10" (20–25cm)	Zones 4–9
'Rosafeder' ('Rosa Feder', 'Pink Feather')	Frilly mauve-pink, blue foliage, long-lived	Zones 4–9
'Rose de Mai'	19th century, creamy mauve, long bloom, 15" (38cm) blue foliage	Zones 4–9
'Spring Beauty Strain'	Classic cottage pink, single, rose shades, to 16" (41cm)	Zones 3–9
'Sweetheart Abbey'	Semidouble deep rose, flecked white, 12–16" (30–41cm)	Zones 4–9
'Tiny Rubies'	Minute double spicy rose carnations, to 8" (20cm)	Zones 5–8
'Ursula Le Grove' ('Ursula La Grave')	19th century, single white marked maroon, 12" (30cm)	Zones 4–9

Perfumed Species Pinks

D. arenarius	Sand pink, 4–11" (10–28cm) tall, ethereal white, reblooms	Zones 3–8
D. gratianopolitanus	Cheddar pink, English native, 2–12" (5–30cm), rose	Zones 3–8
D. hispanicus	Spanish pink, fringed, light pink-white, to 8" (20cm)	Zones 6–10
D. petraeus Noeanus (D. Noeanus)	White alpine, spiny green foliage, luscious scent	Zones 3–8
D. plumarius, Single Cottage	Fringed with contrasting "eye"	Zones 3–9
D. × 'Rainbow Loveliness'	Deeply fringed pale pastels, green foliage, 18" (45cm)	Zones 3–9
D. squarrosus	White lacy ethereal flowers	Zones 5–9
D. superbus	Superb pink, fringed pastels, likes semishade	Zones 3–8

Lilacs (*Syringa* spp.) come by their fragrance honestly; they are members of the olive family, to which the jasmines, forsythias, and scented osmanthus also belong.

Many of my favorite fragrant shrubs are in bloom during pinks season, notably the mock orange (*Philadelphus* spp.), the lilac (*Syringa* spp.), and lavender. Botanically speaking, lavender is a xerophyte, a plant that evolved to survive dry conditions. I have seen old lavender plantings bloom without regular supplemental water at the edge of a Santa Fe parking lot. *Lavandula angustifolia* is the English lavender, "lavender vera," and "spike lavender" you read about in old herbals. I grow *L. angustifolia* 'Munstead', which has rather small leaves and largish blue-lilac flowers; 'Twickel Purple', a slow grower for me, with darker flowers than 'Munstead' (it is said to be an old cultivar); 'Jean Davis', which flowers in an anemic lilac-pink that I do not like (although there is nothing wrong with its fragrance); and a white. All provide me with more lavender for sachets than I can possibly use in a year, and I give them absolutely no care beyond occasional pruning and a desultory side-dressing of organic 5-10-5 fertilizer every other year or so when I think of it. You who attempt to grow lavender upon acid soils would do well to give your plants absolutely the hottest, driest site you can find, and to sweeten them with horticultural lime every year.

Have you grown mignonette (*Reseda odorata*)? It looks like a weed and smells like heaven, but not a Victorian heaven. Its fragrance is too resinous for that, too Eastern, too tangy, too much like sap bursting in a forest of deodars. Some liken it to the scent of violets or raspberries, erroneously, in my opinion, although it has the nose-stuffing quality of the first and the freshness of the second. If you have ever smelled a grapevine in bloom, you will have some idea of what mignonette in flower smells like, though not much. The plants are unprepossessing. Your first impression will be of something green that would be about a foot (30cm) tall if it were not lolling, its stems terminating in small, decidedly unshowy panicles of yellowish green or yellowish gray and white, sometimes tinged brownish red. The flowers are vaguely reminiscent of young cockleburs without the stickers. And that is all there is to mignonette, until you bend close (and you will not even have to do this if the wind is in the right direction). The scent will drape itself over you: green, sweet, slightly sweaty, insistent, very exciting, absolutely French. "Littlest dainty one" (an approximate translation of the name) seems remarkably inappropriate. To have it, you must sow it every year; it is an annual.

Mignonette adds nose allure to window boxes and half-barrels, interplanted with any sun-lover of brilliant color and sturdy architecture. I like interplanting it with red, bronze, orange, and yellow flowers, like salvias (try 'Lady in Red'); snapdragons (use taller types, like *Antirrhinum major* 'Rocket Bronze'); the taller zinnias (such as *Zinnia elegans* 'Scarlet Splendor'); the taller orange *Tagetes* marigolds; and yellow, orange, or red miniature roses. Mignonette also looks smashing with blue *Salvia farinacea* and the green nicotianas: twenty-inch (51cm)-tall green nicotiana 'Nicki Lime' or the one-foot (30cm)-tall 'Domino Lime Green'.

Named from the Latin word *lavare,* "to wash," lavender (left) has scented bathwater since Roman times, and remains a favorite in perfumes, sachets, and potpourris. Mignonette, below, possesses a heady scent that makes up for its rather homely appearance.

Another star of summer is the jasmine tobacco (*Nicotiana alata*). It is few-branched, with huge, gorgeous, sticky, oval to spoon-shaped pale green leaves, held in a clump two feet (60cm) wide. It is topped with two- to four-foot (60cm to 1.2m) bloom spikes night after night throughout the summer. Each blossom is a five-lobed trumpet, seeming pure white at first glance; at second glance, touched filmiest green on the outside of the trumpet. Its flowers open very quickly in deep shade or at sunset, parting pointed lips into a star so deliciously perfumed that it makes hawk moths go mad for miles around. All this grows from seed the size of a cigarette ash.

When sunlight strikes, the jasmine tobacco fades, each blossom drooping in exhaustion until the plant looks like nothing more than a gargantuan wilted petunia. Come late afternoon shadow and evening, however, the flowers perk right up again, ready for action (as it were). Well, they do. All this brings to mind an Edna St. Vincent Millay poem, which every writer on nicotianas must quote, in which she calls *N. alata* "dumb sweet nicotine...which wakes and utters her fragrance/In a garden sleeping."

The closely related woodland tobacco, *N. sylvestris*, is well worth growing, too. It makes a much-branched, four- to six-foot (1.2 to 1.8m) -tall shrub, with deeply lobed, wrinkly,

The woodland tobacco (***Nicotiana sylvestris***) sends its stars skyward in a late summer border. The sweet-scented tobaccos bloom four to seven feet (1.2 to 2.1m) tall in one season from seed no bigger than a pinhead.

If wallflowers are the Aphrodite of the cabbage family, then stocks (*Matthiola* spp.) must be the Ares: the slight scent of corruption enlivens their musky perfume.

blue-gray leaves. It is fragrant enough for anybody, but its chief charm is the way it holds its blossoms: in bursting clusters, like white fireworks. This gives the plant a slightly comical air, as though Dr. Seuss had had something to do with designing it. But it is very pretty, and I always grow a few. Do bear in mind when you are sowing the infinitesimal seeds that a single mature plant can reach the size of a rosebush.

Stocks (*Matthiola* spp.) are vaguely related to broccoli, sporting gray-green foliage, spikes of double or single pastel flowers, and an odd, sweet, disturbing scent, a bit rank, like that of aging hyacinths. Louise Beebe Wilder, in *The Fragrant Path*, describes stocks as reproducing the colors of "old and worn chintzes—old rose, dim purple, delicate buff, [and] cream," which is exactly right. Thomas Jefferson cultivated a strain of them at Monticello early in the eighteenth century. It was not until I moved to Santa Fe's absurd climate that I attempted them, with no great hope of success, and I was startled at how easily they flourish here.

The genus *Matthiola* honors the Italian physician-botanist Pierandrea Mattioli (1500–1577). It contains about fifty species of branching annual or biennial herbs. For cottage gardeners there are two important species: *M. incana*, the day-scented stock,

A night-blooming relative of the familiar morning glory, moonvine covers itself in large, fragrant, alabaster flowers. Each bloom lasts only one night, but another waits to take its place the next evening, so the vine continues to flower until cool autumn nights arrive.

from which most of the garden forms are derived, and *M. longipetala*, the night-scented stock. In summer *M. longipetala* produces single flowers on limp stems ranging in color from whitish to pale lilac to brownish; I have seen only the lilac. During the day they droop, like jasmine tobacco; at night they open their simple crucifer's petals and pour forth a sweet scent with none of the rank undertone of *M. incana*. They are good for pots and small nosegays (they barely reach a foot [30cm] in height).

Of *M. incana* strains, my favorite is a form of the annual summer-flowering, or ten-week, stock, the 'Excelsior Mammoth Column' stocks. 'Excelsior Column' is the tallest reliable garden variety, growing to two feet (60cm) or more; when you cut the central wand, the

plants sprout blooming sideshoots to compensate. I sow the seeds indoors under lights in February for earliest bloom and transplant them to my cold frame by late March or early April. They come in mixed colors as well as separates; in addition to the usual flawless cream-white, matte purple, and rose, there is a gorgeous chamois, an exciting dark, bright crimson-red, and an entrancing blush salmon.

Despite some catalog claims, no seed strain of stocks comes 100 percent double. The gardening books say you can tell the singles from the doubles early on in the seedling stage by lowering the temperature around the flats to around 55°F (13°C) for a week or so until some seedlings appear darker than others. The darker seedlings will bear single flowers and should be snipped off at the base. That's the theory, at any

rate; I have tried it, moving my flats to the coolest part of the propagation room and agonizing over minute gradations in greens. I always end up with a number of singles flowering among my doubles. It doesn't much matter. Even the singles are beautiful, with an airy charm like dame's rocket, good as bouquet filler and sometimes possessing a scent more sweet, if less strong, than the doubles.

I am out of space again, I see, and I have not yet discussed my scented vines: the precious moonvine (*Ipomoea alba*), with its pure white flying saucers; the irrepressible Hall's honeysuckle (*Lonicera japonica* 'Halliana'), which blooms for me all summer with incomparable sweetness; silver-lace vine (*Polygonum aubertii*), with its late summer mignonettelike perfume; *Clematis paniculata*, with its wild grape

A Garden of Fragrance

*Follow this design for a fragrant garden, or experiment with your own favorite scented plants.
Hyacinths, narcissis, and fragrant tulips should be interplanted throughout*

1. *Stocks* (Matthiola incana)
2. *Cottage pinks* (Dianthus plumarius)
3. *Evening stocks* (Matthiola longipetala)
4. *Sweet sultan* (Centaurea moschata)
5. *Wallflowers* (Erysimum cheiri)
6. *Jasmine tobacco* (Nicotiana alata)

7. *Mignonette* (Reseda odorata)
8. *Oriental lilies* (Lilium spp.)
9. *Lavender* (Lavandula angustifolia)
10. *Honeysuckle* (Lonicera spp.)
11. *Summer phlox* (Phlox paniculata)
12. *Rose* (Rosa spp.)

13. *Sweet-pea* (Lathyrus odoratus) *followed by moon-vine* (Ipomoea alba)
14. *Sweet scabious* (Scabiosa atropurpurea)
15. *Dame's rocket* (Hesperis matronalis)
16. *Sweet marjoram* (Origanum majorana)

17. *Fragrant daylily* (Hemerocallis spp.)
18. *Fragrant bearded iris* (Iris × germanica)
19. *Lavender* (Lavandula angustifolia)
20. *'Rainbow Loveliness' dianthus* (Dianthus 'Rainbow Loveliness')

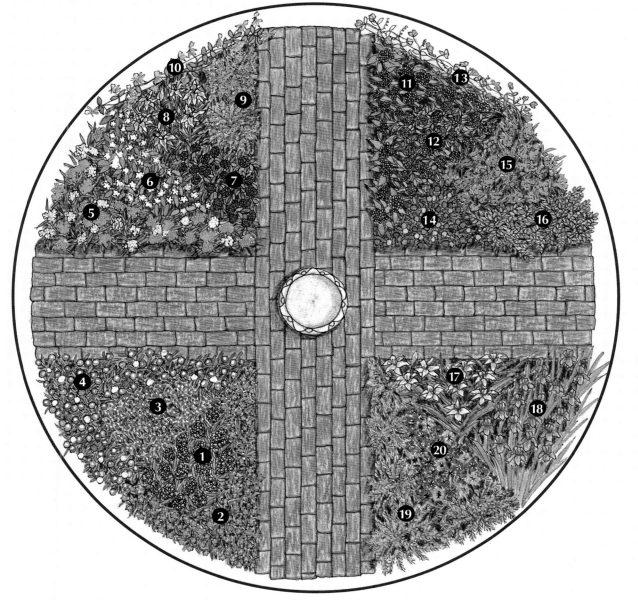

perfume and furry seedheads; and my precious jasmines, now lost to me since my move downzone. I have not spoken of datura (*Datura stramonium*), of Martian seductiveness; or of my frost-tender herbs, which I stick in anywhere there is room: sweet marjoram (*Origanum majorana*), essential for chicken and sleep pillows; my miniature mounding basil (*Ocimum basilicum* 'Minimum'), which looks like a teeny topiary and makes celestial pesto; my caraway-scented thyme (*Thymus herba-barona*) and wee Corsican mint (*Mentha requienii*);

scarlet-flowered pineapple-scented sage (*Salvia rutilans*); the fruit-cup scented *Salvia dorisiana*; and the scented geranium *Pelargonium* × 'Attar of Roses', the leaves of which I use to bolster my rose potpourri. Whole gardens can be given to these wondrous things, and I can mention them only in passing.

So at the last, here, we are left with the lilies, which somebody has called the world's most expensive annuals. Because of comments like this, I avoided growing lilies for years; but really, what do the common sorts need but a

rich, loamy, well-drained, neutral to slightly acidic soil, like tomatoes or roses? The brilliant short Asiatics, available through any garden center or catalog, are unscented but indestructible; give them your best sun, then leave them be.

For fragrance grow the Trumpets, which bloom in July and look like Easter lilies, and the Orientals, which can bloom into September, depending on the cultivar, and look like glorious, big, fat, flat chalices. Close your eyes and choose any. They are all perfect.

I like mixing scented herbs with other plants in the cottage garden rather than putting them off into a plot of their own. Wild marjoram (*Origanum vulgare*), left, billows in off-pink; pineapple sage (*Salvia rutilans*), below, offers scarlet, fruit-scented shish kebabs.

Thyme planted between the stones of a path gives off luscious scent when stepped on. It will happily withstand light foot traffic.

CHAPTER FIVE

THE EDIBLE COTTAGE GARDEN

"The ripest fruit first falls."

—WILLIAM SHAKESPEARE, *RICHARD II*

"The weakest kind of fruit
Drops earliest to the ground."

—WILLIAM SHAKESPEARE, *THE MERCHANT OF VENICE*

Every other autumn, like clockwork, my two old 'Delicious' apple trees lob their ruddy little cannonballs onto the north side of my backyard. I think it criminal of me not to pick up all these apples, cut out the worms, and make applesauce out of them, for these 'Delicious' apples are not of the supermarket kind; they actually have flavor, flavor that could stand up well to cooking. They date from the late 1940s, when my housing development was rural. Several years ago, we thought we would have to cut one of them down, but the landlord had the brilliant idea to prune it, and it has come back with renewed vigor. Trees hang on.

Mother discouraged us from cutting blooming fruit boughs for the house, considering them too potent a symbol of hope to despoil. Here, apple trees flower in a Sussex spring.

Between my back and front yards, just over the fence that keeps my blind husky-mix, Moon Pie, from wandering, someone planted several golden currant bushes (*Ribes aureum*) long ago. They are nearly as tall as the house. In early spring, through my study window, I watch them open reddish buds to clove-scented golden blossoms—blossoms that, pollinated, by midsummer have turned into deep black currants of exquisite flavor. In the autumn, their very distinctive curranty leaves become tinged red. I never water these bushes, or feed them, though I occasionally prune them to near the ground, whereupon the next year they spring up more lush and fruitful than ever. The bushes are at least fourteen years old and pest-free.

In the front yard, against the concrete block wall that marks the southernmost boundary of my territory, my serviceberry whips itself into a froth of white each spring. It is not the wild form of this underrated shrub; it is a self-fruitful cultivar, *Amelanchier alnifolia* 'Regent', known for the quality of its fruit. The fruits, which are best eaten raw rather than cooked, look exactly like big, fat, dark blueberries, though the flavor, sweet and refreshing, has none of the blueberry's acidity. I must irrigate my amelanchier every one or two weeks for it to fruit well; it is not as drought adapted as the golden currant is. But it loves the alkaline loam in which I have planted it. Its fruit is a treasure in the late, hot days of June.

These are not the only fruits in my garden. I have a gooseberry bush that I put in shade—not the best place if you want gooseberries.

Now it is so firmly entrenched I could never dig it up, so I leave the ten or twenty berries it bears every year to the birds, which have a keen eye for the day, hour, and minute of their ripening.

I have better hopes for my yellow-fruited alpine strawberry border (*Fragaria vesca* 'Yellow Wonder'). It is protected from the full blaze of the afternoon sun, because these plants evolved in woodland conditions. I am particularly proud of it because I raised every plant from seed myself. There is nothing more

Gooseberries, below left, and alpine strawberries, below, adapt well to shade and can tolerate some drought. So, of course, can the birds that adore them.

exciting than raising strawberries from seed. From the very first, the seedlings look like strawberry plants, so that you can scarcely believe your eyes; and then when they get big enough to transplant outside, and put up their first flowers, you feel as God must have felt the first time Adam stood up on his own.

Because alpine strawberries do not run, they make wonderful edging and container plants, each forming a little clump that gets fatter and fatter over the years. To do their best, however, they like a well-drained soil, regular irrigation, and a compost or straw mulch so that their roots don't dry out. This small trouble is worth taking. They make up for the small size of their fruit by putting out flowers and fruit all spring and summer long, and the flavor of their fruit is extraordinary.

I note all of this so that you will not think ill of me when I admit that I do not grow vegetables in my cottage garden anymore. This is not because vegetables hate me; I grew loose-leaf lettuce, tomatoes, summer squash, and string beans for several years, trellising whatever I could and hovering like an anxious father-to-be over every baby zucchini. But I am old and fat now, and the older and fatter I get, the less I want to fool with row covers and dormant oil sprays and shade screening and extra irrigation, all the stuff I would need to produce the kinds of results I'd want in my sun-baked, 100 percent organic, insect-ridden rented yard. The books say you can raise all the vegetables you ever thought possible on less land than you could imagine with little or no work, but these books are written by lean

mesomorphs whose idea of relaxation is running backhoe races down at the Grange.

Trust me. Raising food is hard work if you are going to do it right, because most common vegetables and fruits have been so changed by human intervention that they have lost much of

their wild hardiness and resistance to pests and diseases. Consequently, the gardener must be on guard all season, vigilant for the first flea beetle, poised to sound the clarion at the first smear of powdery mildew. There are ways of making this work more efficiently: choose the most pest-

Mixing flowers, herbs, and vegetables together, opposite, is a time-honored tradition, albeit a French one. It is certainly the best approach if you are gardening in a limited space.

Melons in the border demonstrate the joys of vertical gardening. Space can be found for fruit in most cottage plots. So what if melons are cheaper at the market? It's the romance of the thing.

and disease-resistant varieties adapted to your area, and set up a regular schedule of feeding, pruning, mulching, spraying, slug-picking, harvesting, and composting. If all this happens to be the sort of work you love, then of course you will not think of it as a burden. And there are rewards: the incomparable melon, the seductive tomato, the spurting cucumber, the seraphic peach warm from the sun.

Traditionally, edibles and ornamentals are separated in the North American garden, with flowers in front so the neighbors can admire them, and food in back so the neighbors can't steal any. (There also tends to be more room at the back of our houses than at the front, unless of course you are one of those lawn maniacs.) However, having admired French and Italian gardens, in which ornamentals and edibles are mingled, I feel duty-bound to point out that this way works beautifully, too.

If you are going to mix edibles and ornamentals in your yard, the main thing to bear in mind is that the shorter the life span of the edible, the more likely it will leave a huge gap in the ornamental border. So you must have ready substitute plants to plug into those gaps as they occur. Relegate your vegetables to straight rows in the backyard, and gaps won't matter

Pears ripened on the tree and grapes ripened on the vine are miracles of sun, soil, and water chemistry within the reach of most gardeners. But such plants take patience and commitment from the gardener.

much. But in the ornamental plot, there must be some continuity of color, texture, and line, or the eye will be disappointed, if not offended. Also, it is a good idea, as with any planting, to put the tall things in back of the short things. You laugh, but a so-called space-saving bush zucchini plant can put rather a dent in the pansy border. Give things room, and remember: fruiting plants must have adequate light to produce well, and you must be able to get to them easily so that you can minister to their seasonal needs. In short, your edible plants will probably demand your best sites.

In some ways it is much easier to design with hardy food-producing trees, shrubs, and vines than with short-term edibles, such as

beets. You can plant your pear trees as espaliers against walls and put your ornamentals in front of them, as long as your ornamentals don't compete with them too harshly for nourishment. (That's why annual flowers make such good companions to perennial fruiters. Annuals complete their life cycles in a year and seldom possess the horrendous root systems that perennials do.) You can also arrange your larger edibles in island beds as specimen plants and arrange flowers around them. This is frequently done with fruit trees, but I have seen sweet corn used as specimen plantings in some Santa Fe gardens.

Needless to say, a five- by five-foot (1.5 by 1.5m) plot of sweet corn is not going to feed

many people for very long. But that is not why urban backyard gardeners create such things. They create such things to remind themselves that once the world was a soil world, a bee world and bird world and seed world, not the concrete thing it has become. So if your Ruling Passion for your cottage garden is to grow sweet corn, I say do it, even if you can fit in only four plants. And if you do have the room in your yard for more than four corn plants, or two tomatoes, or one bed of lettuce, or two hills of beans and squash, bear in mind that a few plants well grown are worth more in the long run than a lot of plants poorly grown. Don't plant more than you can care for daily.

The lettuce 'Tom Thumb', left, yields perfect miniature heads indoors under lights (I've done it!) as well as outdoors, in or out of containers. Tiny tomatoes are in proportion to the greens. Ideal for the wee diet plate.

This is particularly true for tomatoes. Tomatoes and hybrid tea roses like precisely the same growing conditions, but they do not look good together (I tried it one year), which is why, when I grow tomatoes, I grow them in containers at the back of the garden. Any tomato born may be grown in a container as long as the container is large enough. This may seem obvious to you, but it wasn't to me. For years I kept trying to grow tomatoes especially bred for containers. They had names like 'Pixie Hybrid' and 'Patio Pik' and 'Micro-Tom', and I did not find many of them worth growing or, more to the point, worth eating. Imagine my pleasure in discovering that any standard, full-size indeterminate tomato—one that keeps on growing and setting fruit until cut down by frost—can be brought to maturity and reasonable productivity in a container the size of a half-barrel, or (if you have no half-barrels floating around) even a five-gallon (19L) container. Or smaller.

The rule is: the smaller the pot, the smaller the ultimate harvest. This is because tomatoes have big root systems, and they don't like to be rootbound. This does not mean, however, that you can stick a two-inch (5cm) -high dab of a tomato seedling into a plastic-lined, compost-, sand-, and potting soil–filled clothes basket and expect it to thrive. No, you have to transplant tomato seedlings in stages, or they sit there looking miserable, then rot.

If you are seeding your own tomatoes, which is the best way to enjoy the heirloom strains, start with a very small pot, perhaps two inches (5cm). Good drainage is essential. Fill it with slightly damp commercial potting medium. Sow your seeds. Cover the pot with plastic to maintain humidity. Put it in a warm place. When the tomatoes show above the soil, take off the plastic and put the pot in the best light you have. When the seedlings show their first set of true leaves (the indented, tomatoey looking ones, not the narrow, smooth-edged ones that first come out of the seed), snip out with scissors all but the two stoutest.

Gently invert the pot and tap on the bottom so that the seedlings and soil slide out in

one coherent mass. If there are white root hairs showing near the bottom of the pot, it's time to repot to a one-inch (2.5cm) -larger size. Keep repotting as the tomatoes grow, but don't let the tomato roots reach the bottom of the pot. Repot before they can.

If you are limited to buying commercial transplants, look for ones that aren't root-bound. As this is well-nigh impossible—I have seen seedlings one foot (30cm) high in one-and-a-half-inch (4cm) planting cells—look for younger plants. You will know them from older plants because they will be smaller and stockier and they will not have flowers or fruit on them already. Take them home and gently spread out their roots in their new pot, which (again) should be one size larger than their old. (It is probably not necessary to bury the stem. Although I have found tomatoes eager to root along their stems, I have also found them eager to root from their roots.) Leave as many leaves on the plants as possible, so they can eat lots of light and grow lots of roots.

Tomatoes require at the very least full morning sun; all day sun is even better, with perhaps a little shade from the worst of the heat if you live in one of those broiler-oven places. Water and fertilize regularly. For outdoor plants, mix one tablespoon each of fish emulsion and liquid seaweed per gallon (3.7L) of water, and feed your plants with every watering (be warned: fish guts stink). For indoor tomatoes, use any standard chemical tomato fertilizer and follow the directions on the label. It wouldn't hurt to spray some of the nutrient solution on your plants' leaves every week to give them a foliar boost. Twice a

month, check to see how the roots are doing and repot your plants if necessary. Keep doing this until the pots get so big and heavy you have trouble moving them, then stop, because no tomato plant, however heirloom, is worth a hernia. Continue watering and fertilizing throughout the growing season, and you will be amply rewarded with fruit.

It is even possible to grow full-size tomato plants directly in moistened, fertilized bags of potting soil laid flat on the ground. The Brits do it all the time in their little greenhouses. Just give those bags drainage holes (and someplace to drain into), and shade them from the sun so that the bags don't overheat and cook the roots inside. The bags look like hell, but the tomatoes come out the same, so who cares?

Now trellises, both freestanding and wall-leaning, are fabulous aids to home food growing. A trellised south or west wall can be your only hope of growing grapes or melons to sweet maturity. Even gardeners with more room than they know what to do with enjoy feeling overhung with opulence; and for the artsy gardener, a trellised wall can be a canvas. Not that trellises need walls to support them. Freestanding trellises like tepees, A-frames, and garden arches can extend your garden skyward without marring your landlord's masonry or plunging your bedroom windows into fructiferous gloom.

My first trellis was salvaged chicken wire strung between two rusty steel fence posts. It sagged a bit because I had waited until spring to pound in the posts (clay is awfully squishy

Chives (*Allium schoenoprasum*) combine the satisfying visual impact of the best decorative alliums with gentle onion flavor; all parts are edible.
Opposite, cherry tomatoes trained over an arch make admirable use of space.

in March hereabouts), but it grew great pole beans. It was, however, ugly. The next year, in a moment of wild abandon, I ordered from a garden catalog a freestanding metal-pole trellis that even a gardener as mechanically challenged as I could snap together and set up without tools in less than half an hour. I found it no less ugly than my first effort, and rather more trouble to position in the garden; a free-standing bean tower is about as easy to blend into a garden motif as the Washington Monument. But it, too, grew great pole beans.

A well-grown pole bean plant lends an unmistakable air of virtuous prosperity to any garden. "I will arise and go now," wrote William Butler Yeats in *The Lake Isle of Innisfree*, "and go to Innisfree,/And a small cabin build there, of clay and wattles made:/Nine bean-rows will I have there, a hive for the honey-bee,/And live alone in the bee-loud glade." I should also say that few fruiting plants give as much return for as little work. Bush beans are wonderful, of course, but pole beans bear more abundant, more easily harvested crops over a longer period of time than bush beans do and take up a great deal less horizontal garden space. Many gardeners also think pole bean fruits taste better than bush bean fruits.

Despite this, bush types outnumber pole beans in the catalogs by at least two to one. The disappearance of bean poles from this continent may have something to do with it. So may the ruinous expense of garden-center trellises (which usually collapse under anything more weighty than a hanky). So may the notion that pole beans ripen too late for the short growing season to accommodate them. Yet there are now climbing cultivars that produce pods ready for table in less than two months from planting, such as 'Park's Early Riser' (forty to forty-five days) and 'North-easter' (approximately fifty-five days).

The pole beans most commonly grown in North America are cultivars of *Phaseolus vulgaris*, whose ancestors hailed from Mexico, Central America, and South America. The term "runner bean" is most often used to designate descendants of *Phaseolus multiflorus*. They are best known for the scarlet flowers some cultivars bear (hence the alternate Latin name *P. coccineus*), and they are particularly popular

The hyacinth bean (*Lablab purpureus*), left, bears sweetly scented white or purple flowers that mature to these burgundy pods. Widely adaptable, they'll grow from India to Indiana.

Opposite, a teepee of scarlet runner beans rises above a bed of brightly colored blooms. Runner bean flowers, as well as the beans, are edible and make an elegant addition to salads.

in the United Kingdom and Canada for ornamental and table use. Some forms are marketed as limas, which they are not. The true lima is *P. lunatus* (and a close relative sometimes called *P. limensis*), widely grown in the South. Northern adaptavars are available. The term "half-runner bean," perhaps best known to gardeners in the South, refers to beans with a semidwarf habit; that is, they throw out arms and legs in all directions as though they were going to turn into pole beans (but do not).

Plenty of heat-resistant pole beans exist, but cottage gardeners with warm summers can also enjoy several other leguminous climbers. The yardlong bean (*Vigna unguiculata* 'Sesquipedalis') grows fast to twenty feet (6m) tall, adores summer heat, and produces tasty slender green pods sometimes streaked purple.

Some gardeners top the plants at about eight feet (2.4m) to increase production lower down. Pods can get two to three feet (60 to 90cm) long, but for snap use they are best eaten young, at about eight inches (20cm). The winged bean (*Psophocarpus tetragonolobus*) is a climbing subtropical perennial with an edible tuber as well as delicious three- to five-inch (7.5 to 13cm) -long flanged pods; I grew it in Key West (Zone 10) where *Phaseoli* fail. The hyacinth bean (*Lablab purpureus*) bears gorgeous purplish pink blossoms and reddish purple pods and, though edible in all its parts with sufficient cooking, is most often (and perhaps best) grown as an ornamental.

Pole beans were domesticated from wild types by indigenous peoples long before Europeans showed up, and they do not seem to be

older than bush beans; both have been in gardens since very ancient times. Before European settlers came to the Americas, many indigenes interplanted pole beans with squash and maize (together they are the "three sisters" of Native American horticulture) and permitted them to clamber up the cornstalks as they grew. It is often pointed out by advocates of this triple-crop system that, like all legumes, beans are nitrogen-fixers, pulling this element from the atmosphere and fixing it in the soil to fertilize themselves and anything growing near them (or after them). Others observe that beans are not very good at nitrogen-fixing—nowhere near as good as alfalfa, for instance—and that for optimum yields the three should be grown apart.

If you plan to interplant beans with maize, which makes a lovely specimen group, it is

important to use a shade-tolerant cultivar, such as 'Genuine Cornfield,' also called 'Scotia' and 'Striped Creaseback,' harvested young as a snap or green shell bean; the drought-tolerant 'Ruth Bible'; 'Alabama No. 1 Purple Pod'; and 'Turkey Craw,' a buff-seeded cultivar from the upper and mid-South. These shade-tolerant cultivars are also worth trying if you're a pole bean fan saddled with elm trees (though all pole beans need as much sun as possible and none will do well in full shade).

Choose your bean supports with space and convenience in mind. Tepees, though picturesque, take up more space than pole setups or linear trellises do. In addition, they are widest at their bottoms, where the bean plants are least lush, and narrowest at their tops, where the bean vines grow thickest. The result can be a hard-to-harvest tangle. A-frame trellises also take up a fair amount of room at the base. Another bean-training method is to throw a row of S-hooks over your eave gutters and run heavy twine, pulled taut, from each to parallel pegs sunk into your garden bed. You can affix your twine to bent nails driven into the fascia under the eaves, running the lines down to horizontal one-by-twos anchored parallel to the overhangs. I saw one ingenious wall trellis made of an eight-foot (2.4m) length of white enameled modular wire shelving, set on its end, sunk about three inches (7.5cm) into the soil, and tied to a drainpipe descending from the house roof.

With all that space you're saving by growing your beans in the air, you should have room to plant other crops between and among them. Morning glories may be trained on the same trellis as pole beans, if you don't mind the crowding; so may the fragrant moonvine (*Ipomoea alba*) and the chayote squash (*Sechium edule*). For that matter, 'Scarlet Emperor' runner beans look wonderful with purple-podded beans, and the hummingbirds go crazy over both of them. Base them with scarlet China pinks such as *Dianthus × chinensis* 'Ideal Series Crimson', *Zinnia elegans* 'Scarlet Splendor', or some red salvias for a very pretty picture indeed. In addition, I have grown tall orange calendulas (such as *Calendula officinalis* 'Radio') in front of my bean trellises to hide the bean

Fresh from the tree, juicy, ripe plums are truly a delicacy. The fruit has long been a somewhat unusual but sentimental favorite for jellies and jams.

cots, and all the rest, until it is all that I can do to refrain from placing a very large order. I do refrain, of course, because it takes most fruit trees anywhere from three to six years to produce reasonable crops, and I am a selfish, mean little creature who resents sowing where he will not reap. The hardest items to resist in these catalogs are the dwarf and superdwarf trees. They are usually normal-sized trees grafted onto dwarfing rootstock (though occasionally you can find true miniatures among them), and there is scarcely a yard in existence that could not support at least two.

There is every reason to grow these plants. They do not take up much room; they are fairly easy to care for; they make marvelous specimen plants in half-barrels; they are easy to protect from birds and insects; and they provide the household with a taste of real fruit, warm from the sun, full of flavor and what the advertising people like to call "goodness." It is wise, however, to order your stock from a well-established nursery whose employees can answer your questions. This is because certain rootstocks do better on some soils than others, and certain fruiting cultivars do better in some climates than others. "I live in Zone 6 with -10°F (-23°C) winter temperatures on heavy clay alkaline soil. Which of your dwarf peaches is likely to do best for me?" This is the sort of question you should ask, and the sort of answer

plants' bare legs. Give your beans a good head start before planting their companions, unless you are growing them with corn; in that case, it's the corn that will need the head start.

The trouble with renting is that you never know if any year is going to be your last in your little garden. Some would say this is also the trouble with being mortal. But somehow lease-loss anxiety is more inhibiting to my gardening urges than the sense of my physical frailty, and so I have avoided planting many things in my garden that I would have planted years ago had I known I would be renting this place for so long. I mean dwarf fruit trees.

There is nothing more seductive than the fruit tree catalogs. Page after page, they offer up visions of apples, pears, peaches, plums, sweet cherries and sour, nectarines and apri-

Apple trees, opposite, may be trained as cordons in a living fence around the garden. While this is a beautiful way to grow fruit trees, it is also a demanding one, requiring that the gardener prune and train judiciously as the tree grows. Left, luscious pears dangle from the boughs of a tree grown against a wall. Like cordons, espaliered trees obligate the gardeners to train the trees carefully, but they can be an important space-saving measure in a small garden. Below, Morello cherries (*Prunus cerasus* var. *austera*) tempt both bird and human from their ripening twigs.

you get is what separates the bad nurseries from the good ones. You should also ask if the tree you want requires a pollinator. Consider ordering one in any case. Even self-fertile trees tend to bear better crops when you plant them with a sibling.

Be sure you follow exactly the nursery's instructions for unwrapping, prepping, and planting your trees when you get them home, particularly if your trees are sent bareroot, which is the norm. Many nurseries recommend plunging them into buckets of water and leaving them to rehydrate overnight (the addition of plant vitamins to the water seems to help, too). The important thing is to get

them into the ground as soon as possible. This means you must start preparing their sites *before* you send off your tree order, or you must plan on staying home from work the next day after you receive it. You will need the time in order to dig a good, big, deep hole; mix your local soil with compost, fertilizer, and other additives; perform a test for drainage (most fruit trees hate standing water near their roots); lay out the roots carefully into the hole; backfill; water; backfill again; and mulch. No effort is wasted here, because the entire history of your relationship with your trees is to a great deal determined by how much trouble you take with siting and planting.

This is the case, of course, even when you are planting dandelions, but dandelions and other garden flowers never seem quite the investment that a dwarf white nectarine does the day you plant it. Do not expect it to look like much for some weeks. If you have prepared the site carefully, if you water this deadlooking twiggy creature regularly, and if you have the drainage right, then eventually you will go out to your little orchard and scream with delight at the first purple-green leaf bud. Never mind that ten minutes later the dog, attracted by your cries, will come along and knock it off. Another will follow, as sure as birth and death.

CHAPTER SIX

COTTAGE GARDENING ON DIFFICULT SITES

"What a man needs in gardening is a
cast-iron back, with a hinge in it."
—CHARLES DUDLEY WARNER,
MY SUMMER IN A GARDEN

Anyone anywhere can have a cottage garden, including people in high-rises, but it would be folly to assume that all cottage garden plants are suited to all climates and soil conditions. I have learned this firsthand, since I have gardened on acid loam, acid sand, acid clay, and alkaline clay, in Zones 6 through 11, at elevations varying from sea level to seven thousand feet (2,134m) above. In each place I have tried to plant my favorite flowers, and in each place flowers have thrived and flowers have died horrible deaths. After half a lifetime of this you begin to notice which plants (or their close relatives) are adaptable to a wide variety of climates and which are not. You will notice, for example, that nowhere in this book have I mentioned astilbes.

Astilbes are marvelous plants for the moist, richly fertile, shaded plot, putting up in summer wild plumes of white, pink, rose, red, salmon, lilac, or cream. In Connecticut shade, the astilbes can put on quite a show. But plant those same astilbes in my hot, dry garden, and they will croak faster than you can say "Saxifragaceae." What's an astilbe-loving Santa Fe gardener to do? What any gardener faced with this dilemma can do: change my garden to suit the astilbe, an expensive proposition, or find a similar plume-plant that is naturally suited to my climate and soil conditions. I can think of a number of such plants: the red-bronze to buff feather reed grass, *Calamagrostis* × *acutiflora* 'Karl Foerster'; the lovely violet-blue Russian sage (*Perovskia atriplicifolia*); the pale lemon *Solidaster* 'Lenore'; and the white *Spiraea nipponica* 'Snowmound'. And let's not forget the annuals.

If I could provide them with the moist shade they like, I would grow astilbes (*Astilbe* spp.) for their soft plumes. *Astilbe × simplicifolia* 'Bronze Elegance', opposite, lights up a dappled corner.

Anemones are another cottage flower I learned to do without. The delicate blush-tinted petals of *Anemone × hybrida* 'Queen Charlotte', left, require moister, cooler conditions than they will find in the Southwest.

Cockscomb (*Celosia* spp.) comes in roughly two types: spikelike and brainlike. Left: *Celosia argentea* 'Wine Sparkler', red-plumed and bronzy-leaved, is here paired with Japanese blood grass (*Imperata cylindrica*).

Celosia argentea 'Wine Sparkler' makes glorious red plumes atop wine-bronze foliage all summer on plants to thirty inches (76cm) tall. None of these replacements are astilbes, but they are enough like astilbes in their feathering effect to be useful stand-ins for them. And they're much better adapted to my climate than astilbes would be.

Anemones are another example. My soil is not cool or moist enough for most of them, so despite the fact that I would kill for a spring drift of windflowers (*Anemone nemorosa*) or a

117

cloud-of-white-butterflies *A.* × *hybrida* 'Whirl-wind', I must smother my lust and content myself with a locally adapted cousin, the good old fuzzy *Pulsatilla vulgaris*. And what about my creeping buttercups (*Ranunculus repens*)? One needs them in order to hold the flowers up to a friend's chin for divining her fondness or aversion to butter. Yet not a buttercup marks the buffalo grass lawns of Santa Fe: too alkaline, too dry.

So I have come up with a list of traditional cottage garden plants that seem adapted to most zones and soils. If you're in doubt what to try, try these first.

Snapdragons perform well nearly everywhere. I remember distinctly the day snap-

***P**ulsatilla vulgaris*, the common Pasque flower, is one of the first plants to bloom each spring in my Santa Fe garden. Its violet petals, centered gold, make a mounding cluster bigger every year.

dragons reentered my life. I had just moved to Santa Fe with my partner, Alex, to a small apartment complex on Catron Street. There, in the central courtyard of our housing unit, was a cottage garden of sorts, tended by a stolid manservant, each plant carefully spaced one foot (30cm) apart whether it needed it or not. I barely recognized as snapdragons the cheerful dwarf red, yellow, and orange open-throated paintbox snaps yapping about in tubs, but growing just over the courtyard wall were some stunning white snapdragons of medium height, each with a magenta-purple lip. I know now they were the cultivar *Antirrhinum majus* 'Princess White with Purple Eye', but seeing them for the first time, I thought them as exotic as cattleyas.

In the irritating way of so many cottage flowers, for all intents and purposes snapdragons appeared from nowhere in the literature of sixteenth-century Europe, already well known. When I was a child, my mother taught me how to pinch the upper and lower petals from the back to make the snout-shaped blossoms open and shut. The genus name, *Antirrhinum*, means "snoutlike," and all the common old

Painted tongue (*Salpiglossis* spp.) makes a soft backdrop for the assertive spikes of the snapdragon (*Antirrhinum major*). Horrible yappy superdwarf snaps do exist. I prefer the tall strains, such as the Rocket series, which can get forty inches (102cm) tall under good conditions.

British names refer to the mouthlike quality of the flowers: "dragon's mouth," "calf's snout," and "lion's mouth." This is one of the snapdragon's chief charms, so leave it to modern breeders to desnap it. Euphemistically called "open-faced," the desnapped snaps (like the strain 'Madame Butterfly') proffer lips brightly painted and perennially parted, like those of a slightly drunk starlet hoping to snag a director at a Hollywood party. Some Brits call them "penstemon-flowered," which is sweet of them. I call them "cupdragons."

Have you ever seen snapdragons in full bud? Their spikes seem studded with fat knots of blackish red or greenish cream or pale yellow or slightly bruised pink. These knots open from the bottom up into scarlet, burgundy, white, lemon, gold, orange, magenta, or rose, usually with a contrasting color in the throat or lower lip. The pink snaps used to be pretty muddy, but they are getting better. And sometimes snapdragons are fragrant, exhaling the faint sweet-dry smell of a clean laundry room.

It is a mistake to plant tall snaps—or any other tall spiky plant except possibly yuccas and Lombardy poplars—in rows, like soldiers. Mass them instead, like tourists in a piazza, or dot them around as specimen plants, like those same tourists freed at last from their boring tour to explore the local bars. I grow snapdragons in and among my perennials as a substitute for foxgloves, which will not tolerate my dry alkaline soil. Being spike plants, tall snapdragons look great with blob plants, mist plants, and other spikes. I've backed the tall *Antirrhinum majus* 'Rocket White' with bronze fennel (*Foeniculum vulgare* 'Purpurascens'); paired 'Rocket Rose' with Shasta daisies; and grown 'Rocket Yellow' against a clump of lilac campanula. 'Rocket Bronze' makes an intriguing mate for 'Bright Lights' cosmos, and for cream- or peach-colored nasturtiums.

The bachelor's button, *Centaurea cyanus*, is a grand flower for sandy soils, though I have seen it flourishing in Santa Fe clay, too, so perhaps it doesn't read the gardening books. Yes, bachelor's buttons are annuals, and common. Yes, you need to deadhead them for best dis-

It has been called everything from bachelor's button to hurtsickle, bluebottle to cornflower, but *Centaurea cyanus*— particularly in its blue forms— does for summer what blue flax does for spring. Opposite, flowers that grow in tall spires, like snapdragons—and the foxgloves, delphiniums, and lupines shown here— look best planted in masses or milling about the garden casually, rather than marching in regimental rows.

play. Yes, they reseed like mad. But there are cultivars for every size of garden: wee, medium, and giant. They adapt well to containers, bad soil, dryish sites, and full sun, and unwanted seedlings are easily weeded. Furthermore, the flowers can last five to eight days in the vase if you (1) cut them just below a stem node when fully opened (or nearly so), and (2) stand them up to their necks overnight in cold water. They bloom in true blue (everyone's favorite), pink, white, and burgundy. *C. cyanus* planted in mass creates a misty effect, and looks great with snapdragons, zinnias, gayfeathers, and daisies of all sorts.

A related flower, and just as adaptable as bachelor's button, is *Centaurea americana*, the American basket flower. It is, of course, a North American native, another annual, at home in the central and southwestern United States. Once a popular Victorian annual, it is now virtually unknown in North America. It is called "basket flower" after the shape of its seedhead. Its seeds, which look pretty much like any bachelor's button seeds, only larger, grow effortlessly into vast plants six feet (1.8m) tall by three feet wide (90cm), with huge, softly scented, five-inch (13cm) -wide rosy lilac blossoms with paler centers. In *C. americana* the florets have been reduced to thin filaments, so that the effect is thistlehead-like, or shaving brush–like, soft as swan's down against the cheek. They are produced from late summer into autumn from a spring sowing; deadheading prolongs the show. Bees go mad for them and so do humans: everyone who passes my basket flowers stops dead and demands to know what they are. They are grand for cutting.

I am happy to report that I have found a maroon centaurea that is perennial: Spanish buttons, *Centaurea nigra*. The plants grow quickly from seed, first establishing their strong, gray-green, basal rosettes, then sit for weeks. Suddenly, in late summer, they throw up two-foot (60cm) stalks of single maroon flowers that are very lovely, in a disreputable sort of way of wild centaureas. They last in the vase like their relatives and are said to be hardy from Zones 5 though 10; so once you have a clump established, you will never have to do without it.

There is also that divine annual, the sweet sultan, once *C. moschata* and now reclassified in its own genus, *Amberboa*. The sweet sultan is a priceless treasure, adaptable and tough, yet perhaps one gardener in fifty grows it. The flowers look like shaving brushes, and they breathe a delicate honey fragrance, which tends to be strongest in cool weather, early morning, and early evening. The mixed-color strains bloom in lilac, rosy purple, white, or yellow, though in my experience the lilac predominates. 'Imperialis' is the tallest strain, to four feet (1.2m). 'The Bride' is a bit shorter and is my favorite selection, a pale creamy white that blooms all summer (though it is inclined to flop). A buttercup yellow subspecies, *A. moschata* 'Suaveolens', is shortest of all, about a foot (30cm) tall.

Jasmine tobacco (*Nicotiana alata*) is another flower that pleases in almost any soil and climate. If you are used only to the dwarf bedding nicotianas, with their muddy colors, vaguely vegetal air, and only occasional scent, you must try this, their close relative. The true jasmine tobacco, *N. alata*—which

has also been called *N. affinis* and *N. persica*— is few-branched, with huge, gorgeous, sticky, oval to spoon-shaped pale green leaves, held in a clump two feet (60cm) wide. It is topped with two- to four-foot (60cm to 1.2m) bloom spikes night after night throughout the summer. Each blossom is a five-lobed trumpet, seeming pure white at first glance; at second glance, touched filmiest green on the outside of the trumpet. The petals open very quickly in deep shade or at sunset, parting pointed lips into a deliciously perfumed star.

Jasmine tobacco's native range is from northeast Argentina to southern Brazil, so you would expect it to perish at the first hint of frost. On the contrary: it is a true perennial, and though frost withers its aboveground portions (not the first frost, I might add), *Nicotiana alata* can come back from the roots in Zones 6 and warmer.

And don't pass up *Nicotiana sylvestris*, the woodland tobacco. It makes a much-branched bush from two to four feet (60cm to 1.2m) tall, with deeply lobed, wrinkly, blue-gray leaves, and it holds its blossoms: in bursting clusters, like white fireworks. They are just as sweet as the blooms of jasmine tobacco, and what a sight they would make bordering the path in a moon garden! There is a cultivated form bearing the peculiar name of 'Only the Lonely', but I cannot see the slightest difference between it and the species.

Louise Beebe Wilder mutters about the facility with which *N. alata* matures its sticky, rounded seed-capsules and scatters seed. However, in in my dry soil this has not proved a problem. In any case, the babies are easy to weed out. By the way, it is not generally known that the flowers are good for cutting, proving surprisingly long-lasting in the vase. I particularly like them arranged with the scentless everlasting pea (*Lathyrus latifolius*).

The four o'clock (*Mirabilis jalapa*) is another widely adaptable cottage garden flower. I have grown it on acid sand in Key West, on alkaline clay in Santa Fe, and in acid loam in Connecticut, and everywhere I have grown it, it has thrived. I suppose there was a time when four o'clocks were fashionable. Certainly they caused a stir when they were introduced to Europe from Peru in the sixteenth century, and they were common in Victorian gardens. But by the time I first encountered them, in the early 1950s, they had long been considered an old-fashioned country flower, and now one seldom sees them.

It is a pity. They may have been the first flowers I ever grew, and they possess virtues

Nicotiana, opposite and below, comes in pink, red, white, and green, providing a wealth of opportunities for creating interesting color schemes, like this vibrant red border.

children most prize: dramatic size, arresting color, pleasing scent, ease of care, and a bit of harmless mystery. And they are fun to sow. The dusty black seeds are big, easy for a child to grasp. They are ridged longitudinally, with one end pointed and the other sealed with a flattened knob, rather like a quince. Like sunflower seeds, four o'clock seeds look as though they will grow into something magically substantial, and they do.

The genus *Mirabilis* belongs to the family Nyctaginaceae, along with that marvelous little night-scented flower, the South African night phlox (*Zaluzianskya capensis*). *Mirabilis jalapa* is frequently listed under the common name "marvel-of-Peru" ("mirabilis" means

"wonder"); the species name, "jalapa," refers to the Mexican town of Jalapa and to the mistaken belief that four o'clocks are the source of the medicinal drug jalap ("false jalap" is another old name for them).

The plants, which can reach four feet (1.2m) tall and as wide in a single season from seed, mature into lush, frost-tender bushes with rangy green limbs and attractive, oval leaves. Their flowers are funnel-like, ending in a star of five wide, flared lips and prominent stamens. They open in early evening and stay open until the following morning, or until they are pollinated by night-flying hawk moths. Hence the English common name "four o'clock" and the elegant French "belle-de-nuit," beauty of the night.

There is no denying the beauty of the flowers. Some bushes bloom white, some rose, some magenta or pale yellow or in mottled bicolors; in Key West I found a patch of plants with pure white blossoms and shocking fuchsia-pink stamens. Often different colors will appear on the same plant. Most seed houses sell mixed colors. The fragrance of the flowers, which is said to be strongest at twilight, has been described variously as heavy, citrous, or cowslip-like. My nose finds it sweetly refreshing; but in any case, I have never known any human to dislike it. (It is said that mosquitoes find it repellent.) Do resist the temptation to float the flowers in your punch bowl: all parts of the plant are poisonous.

At our home in Connecticut, Mother grew four o'clocks in a sunny spot on the south side of our well house, catty-corner with the funkia, or hosta as it is now called. When I was five, the

four o'clocks were as tall as or taller than I. They adored the hot, wet, humid New England summers. Their vegetable intelligence impressed me deeply, though I felt a bit cheated at having to wait till afternoon to enjoy the flowers. It is only recently that I learned that they are not annuals, but tender perennials treated as annuals. Their roots develop into tubers, which can be dug up after first frost and stored, like those of dahlias, to produce larger, earlier-blooming plants the next year. Most people do not bother, but simply sow the seed fresh every spring or let the plants sow it themselves.

In any case, it is easy to gather from the plants in the autumn. When the flowers are pollinated, the seed-capsule expands into a little bell that opens to reveal the ripening seed within—one seed per flower. Harvest it as soon as you notice it; the next day it will almost surely be gone, dropped to the ground to be lost in the litter at the base of the parent plant.

Another perfumed species of four o'clock is *Mirabilis longiflora*. I grew it several years ago for the first time, and what a treat it is. The plants look like four o'clocks, only with a somewhat more compact and mounded habit, about two feet (60cm) tall by four feet (1.2m) wide at maturity. The funnel-shaped blossoms are white and end in half-inch (12mm) -wide, five-petaled stars. However, in *M. longiflora* each blossom's funnel-tube is flushed magenta-pink and much attenuated, from four to six inches (10 to 15cm) long. The stamens, too, are elongated, protruding like downward-curved butterfly-tongues from the mouth of their flower. They are the same striking magenta as the tube, and the resulting contrast

As a child I was crushed to learn that four-o'clocks (*Mirabilis jalapa*), opposite, open not at 4:00 AM or PM, but generally toward dusk, when they release their lemony perfume. Plants will die back in frost, but they form tubers which can be dug in autumn and replaced come spring. Few gardeners bother, as the plants are effortless from seed. All-American blanket flower (*Gaillardia* spp.) comes in annual and perennial forms. *Gaillardia* × *grandiflora* 'Kobold', pictured at right, blossoms nonstop all summer on sixteen-inch (41cm) plants. It is as hardy as rocks and will return every year.

with the white of the petals is extremely attractive. The plants bloom from midsummer (if started early) until frost, and unlike the four o'clock, *M. longiflora* is said to be root-hardy to Zone 5. It certainly has proved itself alarmingly tough in my garden, springing up every summer from its deep roots.

I have seen blanket flower (*Gaillardia* spp.), another native American perennial, growing in dry soils north to south. I love *Gaillardia* × *grandiflora* 'Yellow Queen', which attains heights of nearly two feet (60cm) and bears large, simple, soft yellow blossoms all summer; 'Burgundy', similar to 'Yellow Queen' in habit but a striking brown-red; and 'Tokayer', a wonderful rich orange at thirty inches (76cm) tall. Blanket flowers like good sun, but other than this they are not fussy about positioning or soil. All are good for cutting, and they are a nice change from *Tagetes* marigolds, which of course have been much-loved cottage garden flowers since the seventeenth century.

A word about marigolds: none of them is ugly, but most are so saturated with color that they are difficult to place in the garden; they overwhelm everything around them. I am particularly fond of *Tagetes erecta* 'Gold Lady', which covers itself with rich, deep yellow, fully double flowers all summer atop twenty-inch (51cm) plants. A neighbor of mine plants a border of nothing else every year, and every year it stops traffic. They are really spectacular. I plant mine in front of my bushes of bronze fennel (*Foeniculum vulgare* 'Purpurascens'), so the effect is of burning golden globes hanging in front of dark walls of brown-plum. I also like *Tagetes* 'Queen Sophia', which gives us plants half the size of 'Gold Lady' and intensely colored, joyous, brown-red flowers, their petals edged in thin golden lines. How the Elizabethans would have loved 'Queen Sophia', with its richly brocaded flowers! It goes nicely in a window box with violet sweet alyssum and purple-blue painted tongue, *Salpiglossis* × *sinuata* 'Casino'.

Cosmos is another all-climate, all-soil cottage garden flower. You see it everywhere in Santa Fe, mostly in its tasteful pink to rose forms (*Cosmos bipinnatus*), but its vulgar yellow to scarlet forms (*Cosmos sulphureus*) are just as useful (as long as you keep the two forms apart). Cosmos blooms seem to float on their long stems above the foliage, and if cut just opened, they can last in the vase several days. I have never seen any pest on them. Dahlias, too, do well almost anywhere. It is said that they prefer sandy soils, but mine do fine in a clay loam, pumping out armloads of flowers from mid- to late summer. My favorites are not the dinner plate dahlias, but the small informal decoratives, ball types, and minis. I plant them in half-barrels and have great luck with them until the frost blackens their stems. (One of them, 'Park Princess', is a confection in pink, white, and palest yellow, as beautiful in its own way as a 'Peace' rose.)

Daylilies are said to be widely adaptable, but I have no luck with them. If I did I would grow the scented types, some of which stay open for a day and a night, breathing a clear, clean perfume.

Nor do I have luck with hollyhocks, which grow wild all over Santa Fe; mine get a horrible rust disease as soon as the warm weather hits, so I have given up on them. Instead, I grow *Malva zebrina*, the blue-and-purple-striped zebra mallow; the marvelous purple-red *Malope trifida*; and *Lavatera trimestris*, the annual tree mallow ('Silver Cup' is my favorite color). They aren't hollyhocks, but they remind me enough of hollyhocks that I am content.

Annual cosmos (***Cosmos bipinnatus***) is the perfect cottage flower for sun, particularly in its brilliantly colored 'Versailles' strain, right.

Daylilies of Strong Scent

Name and Description	Height in Inches
HEMEROCALLIS LILIOASPHODELUS: *syn. H. flava; lemon daylily; 3–4" (7.5–10cm) wide lemon yellow flowers; noninvasive*	26 (66cm)
'AH YOUTH': *Wide-branched; rich pink 4–5" (10–13cm) rebloomer; darker eye*	28 (71cm)
'BITSY': *Low foliage; tiny ruffled, creped, 1–2" (2.5–5cm) lemon rebloomer*	24 (60cm)
'BUTTERED POPCORN': *Butter yellow 6" (15cm) rebloomer*	32 (81cm)
'CHORUS LINE': *3–4" (7.5–10cm) pink, banded rose; yellow green throats*	20 (50cm)
'FLOYE COPE': *Ruffled 4–5" (10–13cm) long bloomer; pale pink; green heart*	28 (71cm)
'FORSYTH PEARL DROPS': *4–5" (10–13cm) opal-pink rebloomer*	23 (58cm)
'FRAGRANT LIGHT': *6" (15cm) pale yellow rebloomer; strong scent*	30 (76cm)
'GOLDEN SCROLL': *5–6" (13–15cm) textured gold rebloomer*	19 (48cm)
'HAPPY RETURNS': *3" (7.5cm) light yellow mini rebloomer*	18 (45cm)
'HYPERION': *Large, graceful lemon yellow*	42 (106cm)
'ICE CARNIVAL': *5" (13cm) wide; crimped, ruffled; near-white with lime gold center*	28 (71cm)
'ISAIAH': *Narrow petaled 4–5" (10–13cm) golden orange rebloomer; very vigorous multiplier*	36 (91cm)
'JEN MELON': *Very heavy bloomer/rebloomer; 5" (13cm) melon cream to yellow; best Zones 6–9*	26 (66cm)
'JUBILEE PINK': *Broad petaled 4–5" (10–13m) clear pink; green center*	28 (71cm)
'JUDGE ORR': *5" (13cm) wide clear gold, blushed cinnamon on reverse*	36 (91cm)
'JUSTIN JUNE': *Long-blooming; 5" (13cm) wide; ruffled; bright lemon*	38 (96cm)
'KITTEN RICHARDSON': *Vigorous 5" (13cm) very fragrant rebloomer; peach-pink to cream; lemon halo; green throat*	36 (91cm)
'LAST QUARTER': *Huge, 6–7" (15–18cm) pale lemon yellow; long bloomer*	34 (86cm)
'LEMON LACE': *Lacy-edged; bright lemon; small dark green throat; vigorous rebloomer*	32 (81cm)
'LEMON LOLLYPOP': *Very fragrant flat, round, creped, ruffled, 2–3" (5–7.5cm) mini; long bloomer and rebloomer*	24 (60cm)
'LULLABY BABY': *Full, ruffled, flaring; 4–5" (10–13cm) pale pink-ivory*	32 (81cm)
'ORCHID CORSAGE': *Huge, flaring 7–8" (18–20cm) pink-lavender centered cream; long bloomer*	32 (81cm)
'RAINDROP': *Ruffled mini 2–3" (5–7.5cm) round; light yellow*	16 (40cm)
'RASPBERRY FROLIC': *Ruffled, 5" (13cm), rose-pink lavender; darker halo*	24 (60cm)
'SINGS THE BLUES': *6" (15cm); flat, ruffled; powdery pink-lavender; big violet-blue eye; emerald throat; vigorous*	26 (66cm)
'SPRING LARKEN': *Strong multiplier; 3–4" (7.5–10cm) gold stars*	24 (60cm)
'STAR DREAM': *Long bloomer; flared 5–6" (13–15cm) lemon yellow*	36 (91cm)
'STELLA DE ORO': *Vigorous spreader; rounded 2–3" (5–7.5cm) pale gold; needs extra summer water in dry climates for longest bloom*	18 (45cm)
'SUNDAY GLOVES': *Ruffled; 5" (13cm) very fragrant; near-white rebloomer*	26 (66cm)
'TENDER LOVE': *Pink 6–7" (15–18cm) edged lavender-pink rebloomer; Zones 5–10*	22 (55cm)
'WINSOME LADY': *Broad ruffles, 5" (13cm); pink with small green heart; long bloomer; may rebloom*	24 (60cm)

Delicate flowers that demand special conditions—like the 'Stargazer' lilies and miniature roses at right—are often good candidates for containers. And your garden is definitely better off when invasive plants like the 'Eau de Cologne' mint are confined to a pot.

If you must grow a plant not adapted to your soil, or if you have no land on which to grow plants, consider that container gardening is a traditional country practice, dating back in Western culture at least to Roman days. It was once the favorite way of growing carnations, wallflowers, and cottage pinks, and for the gardener without access to soil, the container may be the only way for satisfying the cottage urge. Because you can customize the soil and nutrients for each container, you can grow everything from blueberry bushes to fruit trees to tropical vines to potatoes in containers, not to mention flowers. And it is enormous fun thinking up combinations. There are only a few rules to container growing:

- If you are growing in large containers, like half-barrels or big plastic pots, put the container where you want it to stand permanently before you fill it with soil. Even soil-less potting mixes get hard to lug around when they are wet.

- If you are placing your containers on a roof or balcony, check with your landlord or someone with a practiced eye for construction before you do anything undoable. You don't want the added weight of your plants to bring down the house.

- Plants in containers dry out more quickly than plants in the ground. You can purchase at any garden center packets of water-absorbing polymer granules that, mixed with soil and watered, will swell up into blobs of clear gel that act as water reservoirs for your containerized plants. The

benefit to using these granules is obvious: you will be able to let much more time pass between waterings before your plants show signs of drought-stress. The drawback is that every time you water, you will need to water twice: once for the granules and once for the plants. If you don't, the polymers will grab water away from the plant roots, which rather undercuts the whole purpose of the operation.

- If you live in a cold-winter climate and are growing expensive frost-tender shrubs or perennials in containers, remember that you will have to bring the containers indoors for the winter. Will you have room for them?

How large a container will you need for what you want to grow? Different books will tell you different things, but I have found that everything depends on the richness of the soil you put into the container and how often you are willing to fertilize. In a one-gallon (3.7L) container, you can grow a single plant of most annual, biennial, and perennial flowers for several years. If given proper attention, a half-barrel can house a superdwarf fruit tree; a standard rosebush; two kiwi vines; two indeterminate tomato plants; a Hall's honeysuckle; three determinate tomato plants; or two square feet of salad greens, alpine strawberries, herbs, or bedding plants.

I have grown a number of plants in my little half-barrels—a wildflower mini-meadow composed of *Campanula rotundifolia*, the pale lilac-blue harebell; *Dianthus* × 'Rainbow Loveliness', with its exquisite soft scent and deeply fringed petals; the small, yellow-flowered

Most cottage flowers can be grown in containers if the pots are big enough, including spring bulbs like narcissi and David Austin roses, such as 'Mary Rose', pictured above.

decorative onion, *Allium flavum;* and a blue-green-leaved Cheddar pink, *Dianthus gratianop-olitanus*. In another, I combined perfumed night-blooming stocks (*Matthiola longipetala*), unperfumed day-blooming Virginia stock (*Malcolmia maritima*), toadflax, tansy-leaved phacelia, and bright red pinks (*Dianthus* × *chinensis* 'Telstar Scarlet').

One year I grew a solid stand of wallflowers in a half-barrel, and they were not only glorious in bloom but also easier to sniff and pick than the ones I was growing in the ground. Once I placed a half-barrel up against a trellis and grew sweet-peas in the back at the trellis line, while in front I planted a lovely double, red-flowered, variegated bouncing bet (*Saponaria offcinalis* 'Rubra Plena'). By the time the sweet-peas were done blooming the fol-

The hybrid musk rose 'Buff Beauty' perfumes this wonderful pastel border. The golden shrub at back is *Viburnum opulus* 'Aureum', the leaves of which age from bronze to gold to green.

lowing spring, the bouncing bet was ready to pop, and by virtue of its cream and green leaves, it stayed pretty all year.

You do know about bouncing bet, don't you? A distant relative of the carnation, it has a comforting spicy fragrance in the evenings, a rampaging tendency to spread, and the remarkable property, contained in all of its parts, to agitate water to a cleansing lather. This could be useful if you spend as much time in the garden as I do.

It is a kind of craziness, surely, that moves us out of our comfortable homes into the garden, where we must dig, sow, plant, fertilize, water, spray, mulch, deadhead, and harvest. Well, so be it. The earth gave birth to us, and we will all return to its bosom some day. So what better occupation for woman or man or child than to coax from that earth plants for food, plants for medicine, and plants for delight, all of which serve to make our stay here more bearable?

The ultimate arbiter of your cottage garden's taste should be you, whether your passion is for sweet chaos or sweet order (but not too much order, please).

APPENDIX:
SOURCES AND RESOURCES FOR COTTAGE GARDENERS

Mail-Order Nurseries

PLANTS

AKIN' BACK FARM
2501 Highway 53 South,
LaGrange KY 40031
502-222-5791; e-mail akinback@ntr.net
Catalog: $3 refundable

BLUESTONE PERENNIALS
7211 Middle Ridge Road
Madison OH 44057
800-852-5243
Catalog: Free

BUSSE GARDENS
5873 Oliver Avenue, SW
Cokato MN 55321-3601
612-286-2654; 800-544-3192
Catalog: $2

CANYON CREEK NURSERY
3527 Dry Creek Road
Oroville CA 959675
916-533-2166)
Catalog: $2

CARROLL GARDENS
P.O. Box 310
Westminster MD 21157
800-638-6334
Catalog: $3

COMPANION PLANTS
7247 North Coolville Ridge Road
Athens OH 45701
614-592-4643

DAISY FIELDS
12635 S.W. Brighton Lane
Hillsboro OR 97123
503-628-0315
Catalog: $1

DIGGING DOG NURSERY
P.O. Box 471
Albion CA 95410
707-937-1130

DONAROMA'S NURSERY
P.O. Box 2189
Edgartown MA 02539
508-627-8366; fax 508-627-7855

ELK MOUNTAIN NURSERY
142 Webb Cove Road
Ashevlle NC 28804-1929
704-251-9622)

FIELDSTONE GARDENS, INC.
620 Quaker Lane
Vassalboro ME 04989-9713
207-923-3836

FLOWER SCENT GARDENS
14820 Moine Road
Doylestown OH 44230-9744
216-658-5946)

FLOWERY BRANCH
P.O. Box 1330
Flowery Branch, GA 30542
404-536-8380

FOOTHILL COTTAGE GARDENS
13925 Sontag Road
Grass Valley CA 95945
916-272-4362

FRAGRANT PATH
P.O. Box 328
Fort Calhoun NE 68023

GARDENIMPORT, INC.
P.O. Box 760
Thornhill, Ontario, Canada L3T 4A5
905-731-1950
Catalog: $4

HIGH COUNTRY GARDENS
2902 Rufina Street
Santa Fe NM 87505-2929
800-925-9387

HORTICO INC.
723 Robson Road, R.R. 1
Waterdown, Ontario, Canada L0R 2H1
905-689-6984 or -3002

J. L. HUDSON, SEEDSMAN
Star Route 2, Box 337
LaHonda CA 94020
Catalog: $1

JOY CREEK NURSERY
20300 N.W. Watson Road
Scappoose OR 97056
503-543-7474
Catalog: $2

LOGEE'S GREENHOUSES
141 North Street
Danielson CT 06239
203-774-8038
Catalog: $3

MEADOW VIEW FARMS
3360 North Pacific Highway
Medford OR 97501
503-772-2169 phone/fax

MILAEGER'S GARDENS
4838 Douglas Avenue
Racine WI 53402-2498
800-669-9956

MT. TAHOMA NURSERY
28111-112th Avenue East
Graham WA 98338
206-847-9827

PORTERHOWSE FARMS
41370 S.E. Thomas Road
Sandy OR 97055
503-668-5834 phone/fax; e-mail
Phfarm@AOL.com

PRIMROSE PATH
R.D. 2, Box 110
Scottdale PA 15683
412-887-6756

SOUTHERN PERENNIALS & HERBS
98 Bridges Road
Tylertown MS 39667-9338
800-774-0079
Catalog: Free

SURRY GARDENS
P.O. Box 145
Surry ME 04684
207-667-5589

WEISS BROTHERS NURSERY
11690 Colfax Highway
Grass Valley CA 95945
916-272-7657)
Catalog: Free

WHITE FLOWER FARM, PLANTSMEN
Litchfield CT 06759-0050
203-496-9600
Catalog: Free

WOODSIDE GARDENS
1191 Egg & I Road
Chimacum WA 98325
360-732-4754
Catalog: $2

SEEDS

AIMERS QUALITY SEEDS
81 Temperance Street
Aurora, Ontario, Canada L4G 2R1
905-841-6226

ALLWOOD BROS.
Mill Nursery, Hassocks
West Sussex BN6 9NB
England
011-44-273-844229
Catalog: Free

ALPLAINS
32315 Pine Crest Court
Kiowa CO 80117
303-621-2247; fax 303-621-2864
Catalog: $2

B & T WORLD SEEDS
Whitnell House, Fiddington, Bridgwater
Somerset TA5 1JE England
011-448-278-733209

CHILTERN SEEDS
Bortree Stile, Ulverston
Cumbria LA12 7PB England
011-44-229-581137
Catalog: Free

THE COMPLEAT GARDEN CLEMATIS NURSERY
217 Argilla Road
Ipswich MA 01938-2617
508-356-3197)

COOK'S GARDEN
P.O. Box 535
Londonderry VT 05148
800-457-9703)

FRAGRANT PATH
P.O. Box 328
Fort Calhoun NE 68023
905-689-6984 or -3002
Catalog: $2

GLASSHOUSE WORKS, PLANTS
TRADITIONAL & UNUSUAL
Church Street
Stewart OH
614-662-2142

HEIRLOOM OLD GARDEN ROSES
24062 N.E. Riverside Drive
St. Paul, OR 97137
503-538-1576

J. L. HUDSON, SEEDSMAN
Star Route 2, Box 337
LaHonda CA 94020
Catalog: $1

JOHNNY'S SELECTED SEEDS
Foss Hill Road
Albion ME 04910-9731
207-437-4301
Catalog: Free

OAKES DAYLILIES
8204 Monday Road
Corryton TN 37721
800-532-9545

OLD HOUSE GARDENS ANTIQUE BULBS
536 Third Street
Ann Arbor MI 48103-4957
313-995-1486

OREGON EXOTICS RARE FRUIT NURSERY
1065 Messinger Road
Grants Pass OR 97527
503-846-7578

RICHTER'S: CANADA'S HERB SPECIALISTS
Goodwood, Ontario
Canada L0C 1A0
416-640-6677

ROSE HILL HERBS & PERENNIALS
Route 4, Box 377
Amherst VA 24521
804-277-8030

SELECT SEEDS
180 Stickney Road
Union CT 06076-4617
203-684-9310
Catalog: Free

SONOMA ANTIQUE APPLE NURSERY
4395 Westside Road
Healdsburg CA 95448
707-433-6420

STOKES SEEDS INC.
Box 548
Buffalo NY 14240-0548
716-695-6980)
Catalog: Free

THOMPSON & MORGAN INC.
P.O. Box 1308
Jackson NJ 08527-0308
908-363-2225
Catalog: Free

VAN ENGELEN BULBS
23 Tulip Drive
Bantam CT 06750
860-567-8734

W. ATLEE BURPEE & CO.
Warminster PA 18974
800-333-5808
Catalog: Free

FURNITURE AND GARDEN ACCENTS

ALPINE MILLWORKS
1231 West Lehigh
Englewood, CO 80110
303-761-6334

ANDERSON DESIGN
P.O. Box 4057-C
Bellingham, WA 98227
800-947-7697

BERRY HILL LIMITED
75 Burwell Road
St. Thomas, Ontario
Canada N5P 3RS
519-631-0480

CHARLESTON BATTERY BENCH, INC.
191 King Street
Charleston, SC 29401
803-722-3842

CONTRY CASUAL
17317 Germantown Road
Germantown, MD 20874-2999
301-540-0040

FLORENTINE CRAFTSMEN, INC.
46-24 28th Street
Long Island City, NY 11101
800-876-3567

GARDENERS EDEN
P.O. Box 7307
San Francisco, CA 94120-7307
800-822-9600

HERITAGE GARDEN HOUSES
311 Seymour Street
Lansing, MI 48933

KINSMAN COMPANY
River Road
Point Pleasant, PA 18950
800-733-4146

LANGENBACH
Department L63100
P.O. Box 483
Lawndale, CA 90260-6320
800-362-4490

LAZY HILL FARM DESIGNS
P.O. Box 235
Lazy Hill Road
Colerain, NC 27924
919-356-2828

SMITH & HAWKEN
P.O. Box 6900
2 Arbor Lande
Florence, KY 41022-6900
800-776-3336

TOOLS AND GARDENING SUPPLIES

AGE-OLD ORGANICS
P.O. Box 1556
Boulder, CO 80306
800-748-3474

ALSTO'S HANDY HELPERS
P.O. Box 1267
Galesburg, IL 61402
800-447-0048

ARBICO
P.O. Box 4247 CRB
Tucson, AZ 85738-1247
800-827-BUGS

BETTER YIELD INSECTS AND GARDEN HOUSES
1302 Highway 2, RR 3
Site 4, Box 48
Belle River, Ontario
Canada N0R 1A0
519-727-6108

DAN'S GARDEN SHOP
5821 Woodwinds Circle
Frederick, MD 21701
301-695-5966

EARLEE, INC.
2002 Highway 62
Jeffersonville, IN 47130-3556
812-282-9134

GARDENER'S EDEN
P.O. Box 7307
San Francisco, CA 94120-7307
800-822-9600

GARDENER'S SUPPLY COMPANY
128 Intervale Road
Burlington, VT 05401-2804
800-863-1700

GARDENS ALIVE!
5100 Schenley Place
Lawrenceburg, IN 47025
812-537-8650

HARMONY FARM SUPPLY AND NURSERY
P.O. Box 460
Grafton, CA 95444
707-823-9125

THE LADYBUG CO.
8706 Oro-Quincy Highway
Berry Creek, CA 95916
916-589-5227

LEE VALLEY TOOLS, LTD.
P.O. Box 5
Tremont, IL 61568
309-925-5262

LEHMAN'S
P.O. Box 41
One Lehman Circle
Kidron, OH 44636-0041
216-857-5757

MELLINGER'S
2310 West South Range Road
North Lima, OH 44452-9731
800-321-7444

NATURAL GARDENER'S CATALOG
8648 Old Bee Caves Road
Austin, TX 78735
800-320-0724

NATURE'S CONTROL
P.O. Box 35
Medford, OR 97501
541-899-8318

OZARK HANDLE & HARDWARE
P.O. Box 390
Main Street
Eureka Springs, AR 72632
501-253-6888

PEACEFUL VALLEY FARM & GARDEN SUPPLY
P.O. Box 2209
Grass Valley, CA 95945
916-272-4769

Smith & Hawken
P.O. Box 6900
2 Arbor Lande
Florence, KY 41022-6900
800-776-3336

Valley Oak Tool Co.
448 West Second Avenue
Chico, CA 95926
916-342-6188

Bibliography

BOOKS

ON GARDENING

Jekyll, Gertrude. *Colour Schemes for the Flower Garden*. Suffolk, U.K.: Antique Collectors' Club Ltd.

Michell, Henry. *The Essential Earthman: Henry Mitchell on Gardening*. NewYork: Farrar Straus Giroux.

Mitchell, Henry. *One Man's Garden*. New York: Houghton Mifflin Co., 1990.

ON PLANTS

Brenzel, Kathleen N., editor. *The Sunset Western Garden Book*. California: Sunset Publishing Co.

Brickell, Christopher, and Zuk, Judith D., editors-in-chief. *The American Horticultural Society A-Z Encyclopedia of Garden Plants*. New York: DK Publishing.

Clausen, Ruth Rogers, and Ekstrom, Nicolas H. *Perennials for American Gardens*. New York: Random House.

deBray, Lys. *Lys de Bray's Manual of Old-Fashioned Flowers*. Yeovil, Somerset, U.K.: The Oxford Illustrated Press, 1984.

Griffiths, Mark, editor. *The New Royal Horticultural Society Dictionary Index of Garden Plants*. Portland: Timber Press, 1994.

Griffiths, Trevor. *The Book of Classic Old Roses*. London: The Penguin Group, 1988.

Griffiths, Trevor. *The Book of Old Roses*. London: Michael Joseph Ltd., 1984.

Lane, Clive. *Cottage Garden Annuals*. Newton Abbot, Devon, U.K.: David & Charles, 1997.

Loewer, Peter. *The Evening Garden: Flowers and Fragrance from Dusk Till Dawn*. New York: Macmillan Publishing Co., 1992.

Phillips, Roger, and Rix, Martyn. *The Random House Book of Perennials Vol. 2: Late Perennials*. New York: Random House, 1991.

Phillips, Roger, and Rix, Martyn. *Roses*. New York: Random House, 1988.

ON GARDENING HISTORY

Betts, Edwin Morris, annotator. *Thomas Jefferson's Garden Books*. Philadelphia: The American Philosophical Society, 1944, out of print.

Burr, Fearing. *Field and Garden Vegetables of America: A Reprint from the Second Edition, 1865*. Chillicothe, Illinois: The American Botanist, Booksellers, 1990.

Earle, Alice Morse. *Old-Time Gardens: A Book of the Sweet O' The Year*. New York: The Macmillan Co., 1901, out of print.

Goody, Jack. *The Culture of Flowers*. Cambridge, U.K.: Cambridge University Press, 1993.

Hill, Thomas. *The Gardener's Labyrinth*. Oxford, U.K.: Oxford University Press, 1988.

Lewandowski, Stephen, editor. *Farmer's and Housekeeper's Cyclopaedia 1888*. Trumansburg, New York: The Crossing Press.

McMahon, Bernard. *McMahon's American Gardener*. New York: Funk & Wagnalls, 1976.

Parkinson, John. *A Garden of Pleasant Flowers: Paradisi In Sole, Paradisus Terrestris*. New York: Dover Books, 1976, 0-486-26758-X).

Scott-James, Anne. *The Cottage Garden*. Middlesex, U.K.: Penguin Books Ltd.

Stuart, David, and Sutherland, James. *Plants from the Past: Old Flowers for New Gardens*. London: The Penguin Group, 1989

Thorpe, Patricia, and Sonneman, Eve. *America's Cottage Gardens*. New York: Random House, Inc.

PERIODICALS

The American Cottage Gardener, 131 East Michigan Street, Marquette MI 49855.

The American Gardener, 7931 East Boulevard Drive, Alexandria VA 22308-1300 (703-768-5700).

The Herb Companion, Interweave Press, Inc., 201 East Fourth Street, Loveland CO 80537.

PLANT SOCIETIES

The American Daffodil Society
c/o Mary Lou Gripshover,
1686 Gray Fox Trails
Milford OH 45150-1521

The American Dianthus Society
Rand B. Lee, P. O. Box 22232
Santa Fe NM 87502-2232
(505-438-7038)

The American Dahlia Society
Terry Shaver, Membership Chair
422 Sunset Boulevard
Toledo OH 43612

The American Hemerocallis Society
c/o Elly Launius, Executive Secretary
1454 Rebel Drive
Jackson MS 39211-6334

The American Iris Society
Marilyn Harlow, Membership Secretary
P.O. Box 8455
San José CA 95155

The American Penstemon Society
Ann W. Barlett, Membership Secretary
1569 South Holland Court
Lackewood CO 80232

The American Peony Society
c/o Ms. Greta M. Kessenich
250 Interlachen Road
Hopkins MN 55343

The American Primrose, Primula, & Auricula Society
  c/o Addaline W. Robinson
  9705 Southeast Spring Crest Drive
  Portland OR 97225

The American Rose Society
  P.O. Box 37
  Shreveport LA 71130
  (318-938-5402)

The Cottage Garden Society
  c/o Mrs. C. Tordoff
  5 Nixon Close
  Thornhill, Dewsbury
  East Sussex, West Yorkshire
  England

The Delphinium Society
  c/o Ms. Shirley Bassett
  "Takakkaw," Ice House Wood
  Oxted, Surrey
  England RH8 9DY

The Flower & Herb Exchange
  c/o Diane Whealy
  3076 North Winn Road
  Decorah IA 52101

The Home Orchard Society
  Winnifred M. Fisher
  P.O. Box 776
  Clackamas OR 97015

The International Violet Association
  Ms. Elaine Kudela
  8604 Main Road
  Berlin Heights OH 44814-9620

The Marigold Society of America
  Ms. Jeannette Lowe
  P.O. Box 5112
  New Britain PA 18901

The National Chrysanthemum Society (USA)
  Galen L. Goss
  0107 Homar Pond Drive
  Fairfax Station VA 22039-1650

The National Sweet Pea Society
  J. R. F. Bishop
  3 Chalk Farm Road
  Stokenchurch, High Wycombe, Bucks
  England HP14 3TB

The North American Lily Society
  Dr. Robert Gilman, Executive Secretary
  P.O. Box 272
  Owatonna, MN 55060

Photo Credits

A-Z Botanical Collection Ltd: ©Simon Butcher: p. 2; ©Anthony Cooper: pp. 40, 91 left; ©Matt Johnston: p. 119; ©Ray Lacey: p. 74 right; ©G.W. Miller: p. 91 right; ©Phillip Wiles: p. 98

©D. Cavagnaro: p. 122

Christie's Images: pp. 26 left, 26 right, 34 left, 34 right, 37 left, 37 right

Garden Picture Library: ©Lynn Brotchie: p. 58; ©Chris Burrows: p. 68 right; ©Brian Carter: pp. 15 bottom right, 87, 93; ©Geoff Dann: pp. 3, 120; ©Claire Davies: p. 10; ©John Glover: pp. 14 right, 21, 31, 32, 70; ©Sunniva Harte: p. 25 right; ©Marijke Heuff: p. 96 left; ©Neil Holmes: p. 88; ©Jacqui Hurst: p. 68 left; ©Ann Kelley: p. 42; ©Lamontagne: p. 60; ©Marie O'Hara: p. 78 top; ©Clay Perry: p. 121; ©Howard

Rice: pp. 101 right, 109, 129 bottom; ©David Russell: p. 96 right; ©JS Sira: pp. 15 top, 126 right; ©Ron Sutherland: p. 54; ©Juliette Wade: p. 35; ©Steven Wooster: p. 123

©John Glover: pp. 8, 11, 12 left, 19 left, 19 right, 20, 24, 25 left, 29 top, 29 bottom, 33, 36, 38-39, 44-45, 46, 47 center, 50, 52, 53, 55, 61 left, 62 right, 67, 71, 76, 78 bottom, 82, 84 left, 84 center, 84 right, 86, 97, 100, 101 left, 102, 104 left, 106, 108, 110, 111, 112, 113 right, 114, 116, 126 left, 128, 131

The Interior Archive: (Peter Woloszynski: p. 6, (Fritz von der Schulenburg: p. 12 right; ©Brian Harrison: pp. 27, 49; ©James Mortimer: p. 48

©Andrea Jones: pp. 14 left, 103, 104 right, 105, 113 left

©Jennifer Markson: pp. 65, 73, 95

©Clive Nichols: pp. 30 left, 64, 72, 81, 124, 125; 28 (Brook Cottage, Oxen); 107 (Cerney House, Glouscestershire); 61 right (Chenies Manor, Bucks); 18, 51 (Chiffchaffs, Dorset); 80 (Eastgrove Cottage, Worcester); 17, 57 right (Greenhurst Garden, Sussex); 66 (Mottisfont Abbey, Hampshire); 13 (Sleightholme Dale Lodge, York); designer/Olivia Clarke: p. 92; designer/ Wendy Lauderdale: pp. 22, 41, 56-57, 130, 132

©R. Todd Davis: pp. 15 bottom left, 16, 30 center, 30 right, 47 top, 47 bottom, 62 left, 63, 69 left, 69 right, 74 left, 75 left, 75 right, 79, 83, 90, 94, 117 top, 117 bottom, 118, 129 top

The Language of Flowers

Flowers and herbs have long had symbolic meanings as well as ornamental and practical uses, and at various points in history, most notably during the Victorian Age, the gift of flowers developed into a complex language. Following is a list of some of the most popular flowers and herbs and their meanings; note that not all flower guides gave the same definitions, which could result in some akward moments if giver and receiver were using different guides.

Chrysanthemum	Red means love; yellow denotes unrequited love; white stands for truth
Daffodil	Regard and chivalry
Daisy	Innocence
Fennel	Strength
Flowering almond	Hope
Forget-me-not	Remembrance; true love
Hyacinth	Sorrow
Ivy	Fidelity; marriage
Lavender	Distrust; luck, in some guides
Lilac	First love
Lily	Purity
Lily-of-the-valley	Return of happiness
Marigold	Grief
Mint	Virtue
Peony	Shame; shyness
Phlox	Agreement
Rose	White denotes pure love; yellow means love in decline or jealousy; red declares passionate love
Rosemary	Remembrance and fidelity
Sweet-pea	Lasting pleasures
Tulip	Red means love declared; yellow denotes love without hope of return
Violet	Modesty
Zinnia	Thoughts of loved ones absent

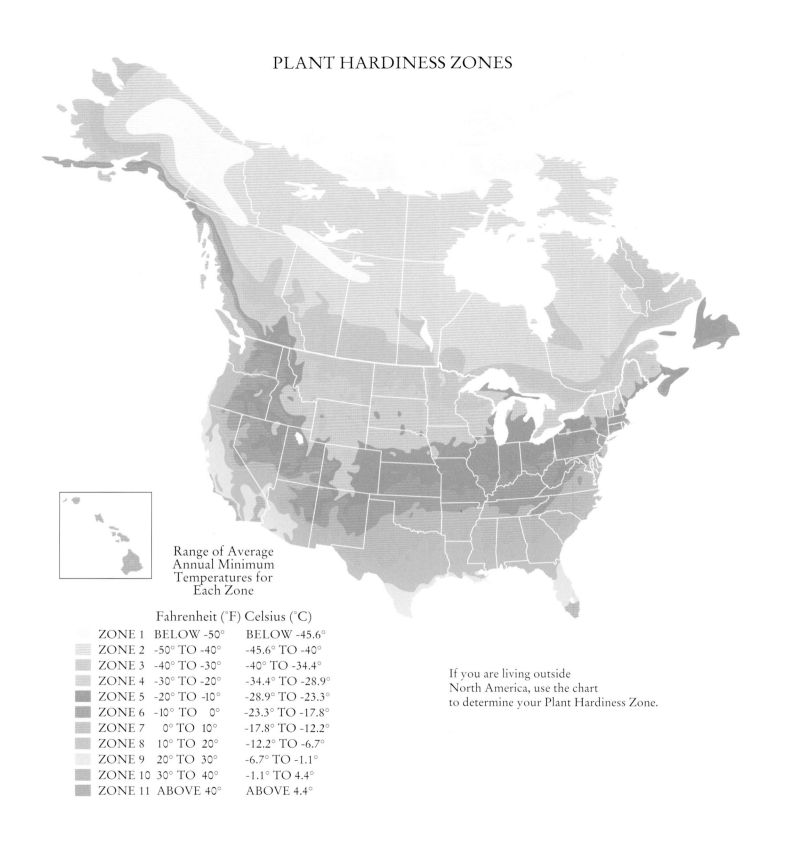

PLANT HARDINESS ZONES

Range of Average
Annual Minimum
Temperatures for
Each Zone

	Fahrenheit (°F)	Celsius (°C)
ZONE 1	BELOW -50°	BELOW -45.6°
ZONE 2	-50° TO -40°	-45.6° TO -40°
ZONE 3	-40° TO -30°	-40° TO -34.4°
ZONE 4	-30° TO -20°	-34.4° TO -28.9°
ZONE 5	-20° TO -10°	-28.9° TO -23.3°
ZONE 6	-10° TO 0°	-23.3° TO -17.8°
ZONE 7	0° TO 10°	-17.8° TO -12.2°
ZONE 8	10° TO 20°	-12.2° TO -6.7°
ZONE 9	20° TO 30°	-6.7° TO -1.1°
ZONE 10	30° TO 40°	-1.1° TO 4.4°
ZONE 11	ABOVE 40°	ABOVE 4.4°

If you are living outside
North America, use the chart
to determine your Plant Hardiness Zone.

Index